BASEBALL CARDS

Text by
Red Foley

PRICE STERN SLOAN
Los Angeles

Published by Price Stern Sloan, Inc.
360 North La Cienega Boulevard, Los Angeles, California 90048

ISBN 0-8431-2471-7

Officially licensed by Major League Baseball

Official Licensee

An MBKA Production

Printed and bound in Hong Kong.

TEAM LEADERS

Hall of Famers

Grover Alexander
Walt Alston
Jake Beckley
Jim Bottomley
Roger Bresnahan
Lou Brock
Mordecai Brown
Jesse Burkett
Roger Connor
Dizzy Dean
Frankie Frisch
Pud Galvin
Bob Gibson
Burleigh Grimes
Chick Hafey
Jesse Haines
Rogers Hornsby
Miller Huggins
Rabbit Maranville
John McGraw
Bill McKechnie (Manager)
Ducky Medwick
Johnny Mize
Stan Musial
Kid Nichols
Branch Rickey (Executive)
Wilbert Robinson
Enos Slaughter
Dazzy Vance
Bobby Wallace
Hoyt Wilhelm
Cy Young

No-Hitters (Since 1901)

7-17-24 Jesse Haines (vs. Braves)
9-21-34 Daffy Dean (at Brooklyn)
8-30-41 Lon Warneke (at Cincinnati)
9-18-68 Ray Washburn
(at San Francisco)
8-14-71 Bob Gibson (at Pittsburgh)
4-16-78 Bob Forsch (vs. Phillies)
9-26-83 Bob Forsch (vs. Expos)

Twenty Game Winners (Since 1901)

1901 - Jack Harper (20)
1904 - Kid Nichols (21)
        Jack Taylor (20)
*1906 - Jack Taylor (20)
1911 - Bob Harmon (23)
1920 - Bill Doak (20)
1923 - Jesse Haines (20)
1926 - Flint Rhem (20)
1927 - Jesse Haines (24)
        Grover Alexander (21)
1928 - Bill Sherdel (21)
        Jesse Haines (20)
1933 - Dizzy Dean (20)
1934 - Dizzy Dean (30)
1935 - Dizzy Dean (28)
1936 - Dizzy Dean (24)
1939 - Curt Davis (22)
1942 - Mort Cooper (22)
        Johnny Beazley (21)
1943 - Mort Cooper (21)
1944 - Mort Cooper (22)

**1945 - Red Barrett (23)
1946 - Howie Pollet (21)
1948 - Harry Brecheen (20)
1949 - Howie Pollet (20)
1953 - Harvey Haddix (20)
1960 - Ernie Broglio (21)
1964 - Ray Sadecki (20)
1965 - Bob Gibson (20)
1966 - Bob Gibson (21)
1968 - Bob Gibson (22)
1969 - Bob Gibson (20)
1970 - Bob Gibson (23)
1971 - Steve Carlton (20)
1977 - Bob Forsch (20)
1984 - Joaquin Andujar (20)
1985 - Joaquin Andujar (21)
        John Tudor (21)

*Pitched with Cardinals (8)
and Cubs (12).
**Pitched with Braves (2) and
Cardinals (21).

League Leaders (Since 1901)

Batting Average

1901 - Jesse Burkett (.382)
1920 - Rogers Hornsby (.370)
1921 - Rogers Hornsby (.397)
1922 - Rogers Hornsby (.401)
1923 - Rogers Hornsby (.384)
1924 - Rogers Hornsby (.424)
1925 - Rogers Hornsby (.403)
1931 - Chick Hafey (.349)
1937 - Joe Medwick (.374)

1939 - Johnny Mize (.349)
1943 - Stan Musial (.357)
1946 - Stan Musial (.365)
*1947 - Harry Walker (.363)
1948 - Stan Musial (.376)
1950 - Stan Musial (.346)
1951 - Stan Musial (.355)
1952 - Stan Musial (.336)
1957 - Stan Musial (.351)
1971 - Joe Torre (.363)
1979 - Keith Hernandez (.344)
1985 - Willie McGee (.353)

*Played with Cardinals and
Phillies.

Wins

*1926 - Flint Rhem (20)
*1931 - Bill Hallahan (19)
1934 - Dizzy Dean (30)
1935 - Dizzy Dean (28)
1942 - Mort Cooper (22)
*1943 - Mort Cooper (21)
**1945 - Red Barrett (23)
1946 - Howie Pollet (21)
*1960 - Ernie Broglio (21)
*1970 - Bob Gibson (23)
1984 - Joaquin Andujar (20)

*Tied
**Pitched with Braves (2) and
Cardinals (21).

Runs Batted In

* 1920 - Rogers Hornsby (94)
1921 - Rogers Hornsby (126)
1922 - Rogers Hornsby (152)
1925 - Rogers Hornsby (143)
1926 - Jim Bottomley (120)
1928 - Jim Bottomley (136)
1936 - Joe Medwick (138)
1937 - Joe Medwick (154)
1938 - Joe Medwick (122)
1940 - Johnny Mize (137)
1946 - Enos Slaughter (130)
1948 - Stan Musial (131)
1956 - Stan Musial (109)
1964 - Ken Boyer (119)
1967 - Orlando Cepeda (111)
1971 - Joe Torre (137)
* Tied

Home Runs

1922 - Rogers Hornsby (42)
1925 - Rogers Hornsby (39)
1928 - Jim Bottomley (31)
1934 - Rip Collins (35)
1937 - Joe Medwick (31)
1939 - Johnny Mize (28)
1940 - Johnny Mize (43)

Strikeouts

* 1906 - Fred Beebe (171)
1930 - Bill Hallahan (177)
1931 - Bill Hallahan (159)
1932 - Dizzy Dean (191)
1933 - Dizzy Dean (199)
1934 - Dizzy Dean (195)
1935 - Dizzy Dean (182)
1948 - Harry Brecheen (149)
1958 - Sam Jones (225)
1968 - Bob Gibson (268)
* Pitched with Cubs (55) and
Cardinals (116).

Earned Run Average

1914 - Bill Doak (1.72)
1921 - Bill Doak (2.58)
1942 - Mort Cooper (1.77)
1943 - Howie Pollet (1.75)
1946 - Howie Pollet (2.10)
1948 - Harry Brecheen (2.24)
* 1950 - Jim Hearn (2.49)
1968 - Bob Gibson (1.12)
1976 - John Denny (2.52)
* Pitched with Cardinals and Giants

Most Valuable Players

1925 - Rogers Hornsby
1926 - Bob O'Farrell
1928 - Jim Bottomley
1931 - Frankie Frisch
1934 - Dizzy Dean
1937 - Joe Medwick
1942 - Mort Cooper
1943 - Stan Musial
1944 - Marty Marion
1946 - Stan Musial
1948 - Stan Musial
1964 - Ken Boyer
1967 - Orlando Cepeda
1968 - Bob Gibson
1971 - Joe Torre
* 1979 - Keith Hernandez
1985 - Willie McGee
* Co-Winner

Rookies of the Year

1954 - Wally Moon
1955 - Bill Virdon
1974 - Bake McBride
1985 - Vince Coleman
1986 - Todd Worrell

Cy Young Award Winners

1968 - Bob Gibson
1970 - Bob Gibson

World Series Appearances

* 1926	* 1942	* 1967
1928	1943	1968
1930	* 1944	* 1982
* 1931	* 1946	1985
* 1934	* 1964	1987

* World Champions

Club Records (Since 1901)

Batting

Runs .... Rogers Hornsby (141, 1922)
Hits .... Rogers Hornsby (250, 1922)
Doubles .... Joe Medwick (64, 1936)
Triples .... Tommy Long (25, 1915)
Home Runs .... Johnny Mize (43, 1940)
Runs Batted In .... Joe Medwick (154, 1937)
Stolen Bases .... Lou Brock (118, 1974)
Batting Average ...... Rogers Hornsby (.424, 1924)

Pitching

Games .... Todd Worrell (74, 1987)
Innings .... Stoney McGlynn (352, 1907)
Wins .... Dizzy Dean (30, 1934)
Strikeouts .... Bob Gibson (274, 1970)
Saves .... Bruce Sutter (45, 1984)
Earned Run Average .. Bob Gibson (1.12, 1968)

1952

Eddie Stanky's rookie year as manager was adjudged a good one when he led the Cardinals to a third-place finish in 1952. As expected, Stanky had some temper clashes with players and umpires but the Redbirds survived and prospered a bit. Stan Musial won his sixth (and third straight) batting title when he hit .336 plus 21 homers and 91 RBIs. The ageless Enos Slaughter batted .300 and knocked in 101 runs while the veteran Red Schoendienst batted .303. As a club the Cardinals led the N.L. with a .267 average. Gerry Staley was the Birds' top pitcher, working to a 14-7 record. Rookie lefty Vinegar Bend Mizell finished 10-8 and freshman Stu Miller was 6-3. Al Brazle, coming out of the bullpen, won a dozen. Ditto for fellow reliever Eddie Yuhas.

STEVE BILKO

CLOYD BOYER

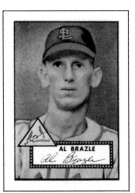
AL BRAZLE

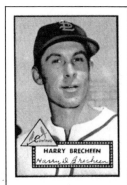
HARRY BRECHEEN

JOHNNY BUCHA

CLIFF CHAMBERS

LES FUSSELMAN

TOMMY GLAVIANO

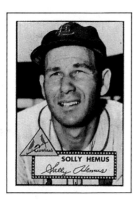

SOLLY HEMUS

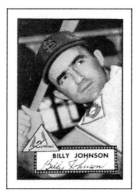

BILLY JOHNSON

EDDIE KAZAK

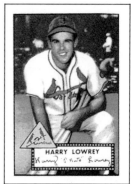

HARRY LOWREY

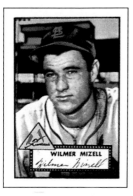

WILMER MIZELL

GEORGE MUNGER

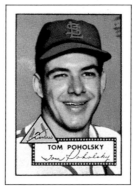

TOM POHOLSKY

JOE PRESKO

DEL RICE

HAL RICE

AL SCHOENDIENST

ENOS SLAUGHTER

GERALD STALEY

EDDIE STANKY

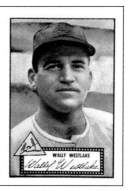

WALLY WESTLAKE

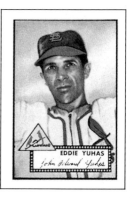

EDDIE YUHAS

1953

It was another third-place windup for the Cardinals in 1953, but this time they had to split "show" money with the Phillies as both concluded with 83-71 records. Red Schoendienst and Stan Musial had banner plate seasons while Enos Slaughter contributed a .291 average and 89 runs batted in. Rookie infielder Ray Jablonski hit 21 home runs and had 112 RBIs. Schoendienst, enjoying the best season of his career, batted .342 while Musial swung a .337 bat with 30 homers and 113 RBIs. The Redbirds' pitching couldn't match the club's offense. Harvey Haddix won 20 games, Gerry Staley won 18 and Vinegar Bend Mizell was 13-11. Al Brazle, out of the pen, was 6-7, but his fellow reliever, Eddie Yuhas, suffered arm miseries that limited him to only one inning the entire season.

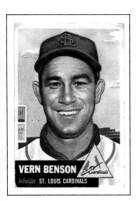

VERN BENSON
infielder ST. LOUIS CARDINALS

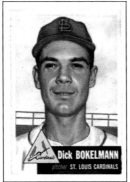

Dick BOKELMANN
pitcher ST. LOUIS CARDINALS

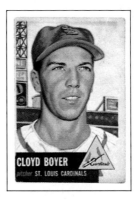

CLOYD BOYER
pitcher ST. LOUIS CARDINALS

MIKE CLARK
pitcher ST. LOUIS CARDINALS

LES FUSSELMAN
catcher ST. LOUIS CARDINALS

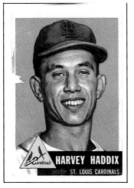

HARVEY HADDIX
pitcher ST. LOUIS CARDINALS

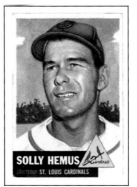

SOLLY HEMUS
shortstop ST. LOUIS CARDINALS

RAY JABLONSKI
third base ST. LOUIS CARDINALS

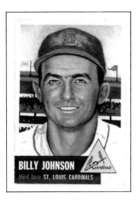

BILLY JOHNSON
third base ST. LOUIS CARDINALS

HARRY LOWREY
outfielder ST. LOUIS CARDINALS

STU MILLER
pitcher ST. LOUIS CARDINALS

WILMER MIZELL
pitcher ST. LOUIS CARDINALS

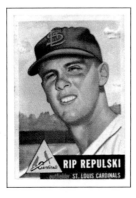

RIP REPULSKI
outfielder ST. LOUIS CARDINALS

DEL RICE
catcher ST. LOUIS CARDINALS

HAL RICE
outfielder ST. LOUIS CARDINALS

JOHN RIDDLE
coach ST. LOUIS CARDINALS

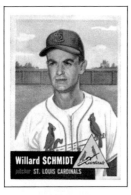

Willard SCHMIDT
pitcher ST. LOUIS CARDINALS

Al SCHOENDIENST
second base ST. LOUIS CARDINALS

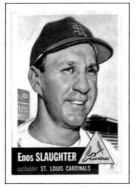

Enos SLAUGHTER
outfielder ST. LOUIS CARDINALS

GERALD STALEY
pitcher ST. LOUIS CARDINALS

VIRGIL STALLCUP
shortstop ST. LOUIS CARDINALS

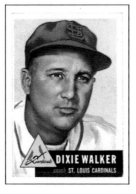

DIXIE WALKER
coach ST. LOUIS CARDINALS

ED YUHAS
pitcher ST. LOUIS CARDINALS

1954

The Cardinals tumbled from third to sixth place in 1954, suffering their worst season since 1938. Offensively, Ed Stanky's club looked like a winner with a quartet of .300 hitters and a league-leading .271 batting average. The pitching, however, was something else. The moundsmen worked to a disappointing 4.50 earned run average.

Stan Musial's .330 average and 35 homers led the team. Red Schoendienst batted .315 and rookie Wally Moon .304. Catcher Bill Sarni hit .304. The staff's top winner was lefty Harvey Haddix, 18-13. Rookie righthander Brooks Lawrence, promoted from the minors in June, posted a nifty 15-6. Vic Raschi, obtained from the Yankees, won eight. None of the other pitchers equalled Raschi's output.

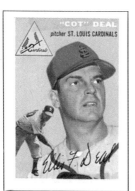
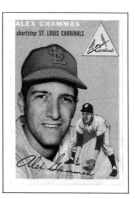
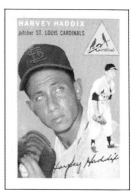

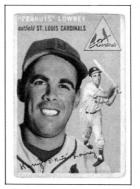

WILMER MIZELL
pitcher ST. LOUIS CARDINALS

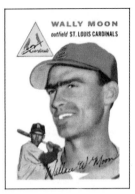

WALLY MOON
outfield ST. LOUIS CARDINALS

TOM POHOLSKY
pitcher ST. LOUIS CARDINALS

JOE PRESKO
pitcher ST. LOUIS CARDINALS

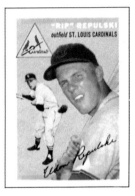

"RIP" REPULSKI
outfield ST. LOUIS CARDINALS

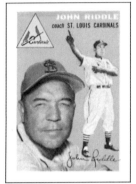

JOHN RIDDLE
coach ST. LOUIS CARDINALS

MIKE RYBA
coach ST. LOUIS CARDINALS

BILL SARNI
catcher ST. LOUIS CARDINALS

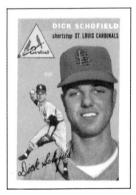

DICK SCHOFIELD
shortstop ST. LOUIS CARDINALS

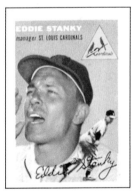

EDDIE STANKY
manager ST. LOUIS CARDINALS

1955

Manager Eddie Stanky was fired in May and Harry Walker, who replaced him, could do little to prevent the Cardinals from crashing into seventh place in 1955. It was the Redbirds' worst season since 1919. The pitching again anchored the club in the second division as they compiled a 4.56 ERA, the highest in the National League. Rookie lefty Luis Arroyo was 11-8 but didn't win a game after July 17. Harvey Haddix ended up 12-16 and Brooks Lawrence 3-8. Tom Poholsky finished 9-11. Stan Musial hit .318 with 33 homers while Wally Moon batted .295. Rookie outfielder Bill Virdon batted .281 while the veteran Red Schoendienst's average skidded to .268.

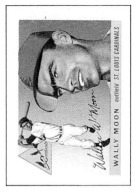

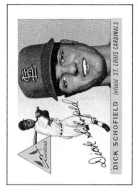

1956

A front-office shuffle that made the controversial Frank Lane the general manager and Fred Hutchinson the field skipper, resulted in the Cardinals rising to fourth place in 1956. The Birds led the league with a .268 batting average but the pitching, for the third straight season, was well below par. Stan Musial's .310 average led the Cardinals regulars and his 109 RBIs was the highest in the league. Young Ken Boyer contributed 26 home runs and 98 RBIs while batting .306. Wally Moon finished with a .298 average. The ageing Murry Dickson, acquired from Philadelphia in one of Lane's many player swaps in 1956, won 13 and lost 11. Tom Poholsky was 9-14 and Vinegar Bend Mizell, back from military service, finished 14-14. Herm Wehmeier, obtained from Cincinnati, was 12-11.

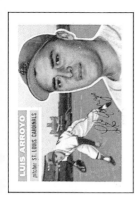

LUIS ARROYO · pitcher ST. LOUIS CARDINALS

DON BLASINGAME · shortstop ST. LOUIS CARDINALS

KEN BOYER · third base ST. LOUIS CARDINALS

NELSON BURBRINK · catcher ST. LOUIS CARDINALS

WALKER COOPER · catcher ST. LOUIS CARDINALS

JOE FRAZIER · outfield ST. LOUIS CARDINALS

ALEX GRAMMAS · shortstop ST. LOUIS CARDINALS

HARVEY HADDIX · pitcher ST. LOUIS CARDINALS

LARRY JACKSON · pitcher ST. LOUIS CARDINALS

ELLIS KINDER · pitcher ST. LOUIS CARDINALS

STU MILLER · pitcher ST. LOUIS CARDINALS

WILMER MIZELL · pitcher ST. LOUIS CARDINALS

WALLY MOON · outfield ST. LOUIS CARDINALS

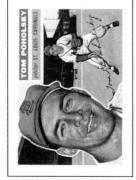

TOM POHOLSKY · pitcher ST. LOUIS CARDINALS

"RIP" REPULSKI · outfield ST. LOUIS CARDINALS

BILL SARNI · catcher ST. LOUIS CARDINALS

  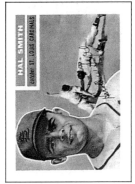 

≡1957≡

The Cardinals, enjoying their finest season since 1949, finished in second place, eight games behind Milwaukee in 1957. Their hitters again led the league with a .274 average, Stan Musial winning his seventh — and final — batting title with a .351 average. He also had 29 homers and 102 RBIs. Wally Moon batted .295 while Ken Boyer batted .265 with 19 homers. Joe Cunningham hit .290 and Del Ennis hit two dozen homers and drove in 105 runs. Larry Jackson posted a 15-9 record, as did Lindy McDaniel. Willard Schmidt went 10-3 and Sam Jones 12-9. Vinegar Bend Mizell finished 8-10 and Von McDaniel, Lindy's 21-year-old brother, went 7-5 in 14 games following his mid-June promotion from the minors.

DON **Blasingame**
ST. LOUIS CARDINALS 2nd BASE

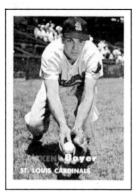

KEN **Boyer**
ST. LOUIS CARDINALS 3rd B.

Cheney
ST. LOUIS CARDINALS PITCHER

ST. LOUIS CARDINALS CATCHER

JOE **Cunningham**
ST. LOUIS CARDINALS 1st B.

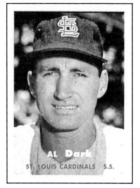

AL **Dark**
ST. LOUIS CARDINALS S.S.

JIM **Davis**
ST. LOUIS CARDINALS PITCHER

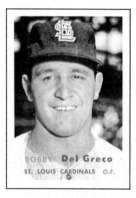

BOBBY **Del Greco**
ST. LOUIS CARDINALS O.F.

MURRY **Dickson**
ST. LOUIS CARDINALS PITCHER

DEL **Ennis**
ST. LOUIS CARDINALS O.F.

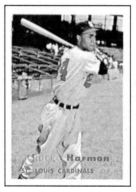

CHUCK **Harmon**
ST. LOUIS CARDINALS O.F.

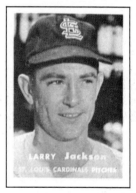

LARRY **Jackson**
ST. LOUIS CARDINALS PITCHER

SAM **Jones**
ST. LOUIS CARDINALS PITCHER

ST. LOUIS CARDINALS

HOBIE **Landrith**
ST. LOUIS CARDINALS CATCHER

LINDY **McDaniel**
ST. LOUIS CARDINALS PITCHER

EDDIE MIKSIS
ST. LOUIS CARDINALS INF.-O.F.

WILMER Mizell
ST. LOUIS CARDINALS PITCHER

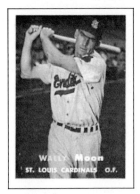

WALLY Moon
ST. LOUIS CARDINALS O.F.

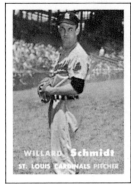

WILLARD Schmidt
ST. LOUIS CARDINALS PITCHER

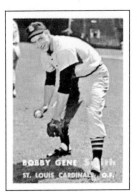

BOBBY GENE Smith
ST. LOUIS CARDINALS O.F.

HAL Smith
ST. LOUIS CARDINALS CATCHER

HERM Wehmeier
ST. LOUIS CARDINALS PITCHER

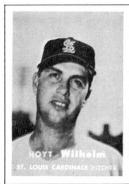

HOYT Wilhelm
ST. LOUIS CARDINALS PITCHER

ST. LOUIS CARDINALS

≡1958≡

A stumbling start, plus a mid-season losing streak that toppled them into the cellar in August, cost the Cardinals any chance of contending for top honors in 1958. The Birds, with Stan Hack replacing the ousted Fred Hutchinson in September, ended up sharing fifth place with the Cubs. Ken Boyer, recovering from a .154 slump in the early going, rebounded to finish with a .307 average while pacing the club in homers (23) and RBIs (90). Stan Musial led the Birds with a .337 average and also chipped in with 17 homers and 62 RBIs. Joe Cunningham swung a .312 stick and added a dozen homers.

  Sam Jones, 14-13, led the staff with a 2.88 earned run average. Jim Brosnan, acquired from the Cubs during the season, chalked eight of his 11 wins for St.Louis. Vinegar Bend Mizell ended up 10-14 while Larry Jackson was 13-13. The McDaniel brothers were big disappointments. Lindy was 5-7 while Von, bothered by arm ailments, pitched only two innings all year.

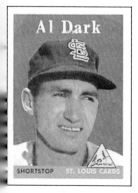

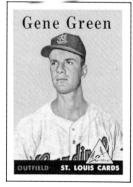

Larry Jackson

PITCHER ST. LOUIS CARDINALS

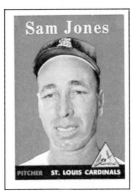

Sam Jones

PITCHER ST. LOUIS CARDINALS

Eddie Kasko

3rd B. ST. LOUIS CARDINALS

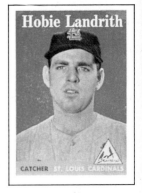

Hobie Landrith

CATCHER ST. LOUIS CARDINALS

Morrie Martin

PITCHER ST. LOUIS CARDINALS

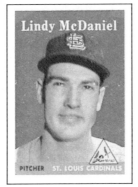

Lindy McDaniel

PITCHER ST. LOUIS CARDINALS

Von McDaniel

PITCHER ST. LOUIS CARDINALS

Lloyd Merritt

PITCHER ST. LOUIS CARDINALS

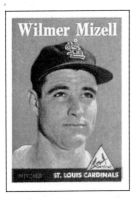

Wilmer Mizell

PITCHER ST. LOUIS CARDINALS

Wally Moon

OUTFIELD ST. LOUIS CARDINALS

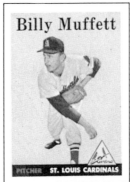

Billy Muffett

PITCHER ST. LOUIS CARDINALS

SPORT Magazine '58 ALL STAR Selection

STAN MUSIAL
FIRST BASE · NATIONAL LEAGUE

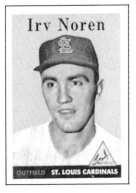

Irv Noren

OUTFIELD ST. LOUIS CARDINALS

Phil Paine

PITCHER ST. LOUIS CARDINALS

Dick Schofield

INFIELD ST. LOUIS CARDINALS

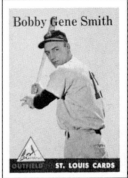

Bobby Gene Smith

OUTFIELD ST. LOUIS CARDS

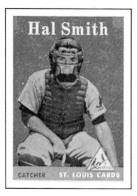

Hal Smith — CATCHER — ST. LOUIS CARDS

Joe Taylor — OUTFIELD — ST. LOUIS CARDS

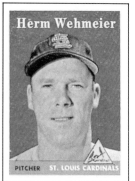

Herm Wehmeier — PITCHER — ST. LOUIS CARDINALS

ST. LOUIS CARDS

1959

Solly Hemus made his managerial debut with the 1959 Cardinals but the club, following another poor getaway, faded following a mid-season spurt, to finish seventh. Despite a .269 club batting average, the Redbirds faltered when Stan Musial batted only .255 with 14 home runs. Joe Cunningham hit .345 but it was Ken Boyer, with 28 homers, 94 RBIs and a .309 average, who provided the power. The pitching never got turned around and the staff's 4.34 ERA was the highest in the league. Larry Jackson finished 14-13 and Lindy McDaniel 14-12. A youthful Bob Gibson broke in with a 3-5 record while Vinegar Bend Mizell, 9-3 until injuring his back in late June, ended up 13-10.

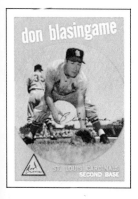

don blasingame — ST. LOUIS CARDINALS — SECOND BASE

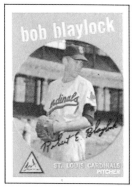

bob blaylock — ST. LOUIS CARDINALS — PITCHER

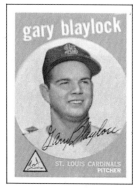

gary blaylock — ST. LOUIS CARDINALS — PITCHER

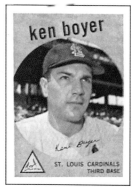

ken boyer — ST. LOUIS CARDINALS — THIRD BASE

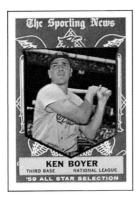

The Sporting News

KEN BOYER

THIRD BASE   NATIONAL LEAGUE

'59 ALL STAR SELECTION

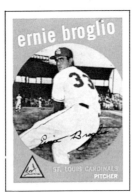

ernie broglio

ST. LOUIS CARDINALS
PITCHER

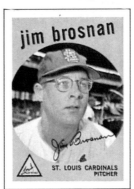

jim brosnan

ST. LOUIS CARDINALS
PITCHER

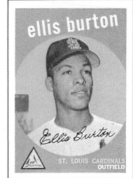

ellis burton

ST. LOUIS CARDINALS
OUTFIELD

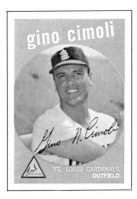

gino cimoli

ST. LOUIS CARDINALS
OUTFIELD

phil clark

ST. LOUIS CARDINALS
PITCHER

george crowe

ST. LOUIS CARDINALS
FIRST BASE

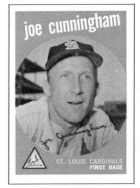

joe cunningham

ST. LOUIS CARDINALS
FIRST BASE

chuck essegian

ST. LOUIS CARDINALS
OUTFIELD

curt flood

ST. LOUIS CARDINALS
OUTFIELD

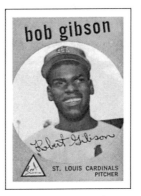

bob gibson

ST. LOUIS CARDINALS
PITCHER

alex grammas

ST. LOUIS CARDINALS
SHORTSTOP-THIRD BASE

gene green

ST. LOUIS CARDINALS
CATCHER-OUTFIELD

marv grissom

ST. LOUIS CARDINALS
PITCHER

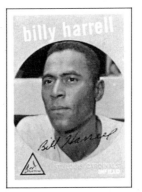

billy harrell

ST. LOUIS CARDINALS
INFIELD

solly hemus

ST. LOUIS CARDINALS
INFIELD-MANAGER

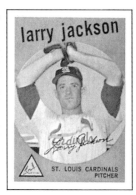

larry jackson
ST. LOUIS CARDINALS
PITCHER

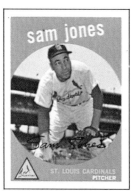

sam jones
ST. LOUIS CARDINALS
PITCHER

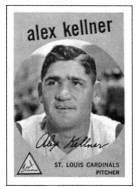

alex kellner
ST. LOUIS CARDINALS
PITCHER

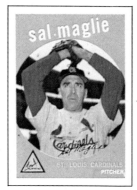

sal maglie
ST. LOUIS CARDINALS
PITCHER

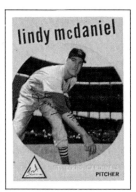

lindy mcdaniel
PITCHER

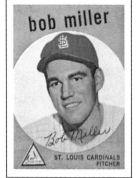

bob miller
ST. LOUIS CARDINALS
PITCHER

stan musial
ST. LOUIS CARDINALS
OUTFIELD-FIRST BASE

irv noren
ST. LOUIS CARDINALS
OUTFIELD

howie nunn
ST. LOUIS CARDINALS
PITCHER

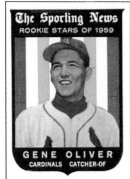

The Sporting News
ROOKIE STARS OF 1959
GENE OLIVER
CARDINALS CATCHER-OF

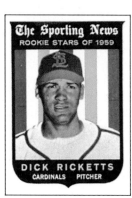

The Sporting News
ROOKIE STARS OF 1959
DICK RICKETTS
CARDINALS PITCHER

bobby g. smith
OUTFIELD

hal r. smith
ST. LOUIS CARDINALS
CATCHER

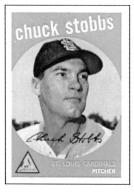

chuck stobbs
ST. LOUIS CARDINALS
PITCHER

lee tate
ST. LOUIS CARDINALS
SHORTSTOP

BASEBALL THRILLS
MUSIAL RAPS OUT 3,000th HIT

1960

The Cardinals, with 39-year-old Stan Musial spearheading their drive, soared from seventh place to third in 1960. Benched in the early going because of manager Solly Hemus' "youth" movement, Musial returned to the lineup on June 24 and went on a plate tear that saw him finish with a .275 average plus 17 homers and 63 RBIs. Ken Boyer, with a .304 mark, 32 homers and 97 RBIs, complemented The Man. Pitching, as provided by Ernie Broglio, Larry Jackson, Curt Simmons, Ray Sadecki and Lindy McDaniel, fueled the Birds' surge. Broglio, with one victory by the end of May, ended up 21-9, the club's first 20-game winner since 1953. Jackson won 18 and McDaniel was 12-4 with a 2.09 ERA. Sadecki was 9-9 while free-agent Simmons was 7-4.

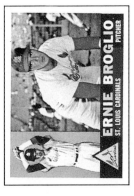
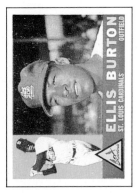

GEORGE CROWE — FIRST BASE — ST. LOUIS CARDINALS

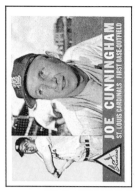

JOE CUNNINGHAM — FIRST BASE-OUTFIELD — ST. LOUIS CARDINALS

SPORT MAGAZINE '60 ALL-STAR SELECTION
JOE CUNNINGHAM — Outfield/National League

SPORT MAGAZINE 1960 ROOKIE STAR
JIM DONOHUE — ST. LOUIS CARDS · PITCHER

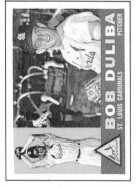

BOB DULIBA — PITCHER — ST. LOUIS CARDINALS

CURT FLOOD — OUTFIELD — ST. LOUIS CARDINALS

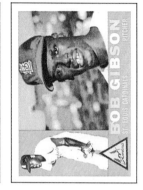

BOB GIBSON — PITCHER — ST. LOUIS CARDINALS

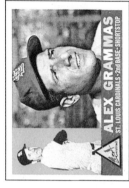

ALEX GRAMMAS — 2nd BASE-SHORTSTOP — ST. LOUIS CARDINALS

DICK GRAY — INFIELD — ST. LOUIS CARDINALS

CARDS
SOLLY HEMUS
MANAGER · ST. LOUIS

LARRY JACKSON — PITCHER — ST. LOUIS CARDINALS

CHARLEY JAMES — OUTFIELD — ST. LOUIS CARDINALS

DARRELL JOHNSON — CATCHER — ST. LOUIS CARDINALS

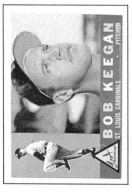

BOB KEEGAN — PITCHER — ST. LOUIS CARDINALS

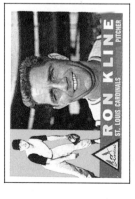

RON KLINE — PITCHER — ST. LOUIS CARDINALS

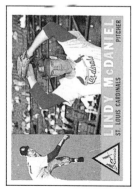

LINDY McDANIEL — PITCHER — ST. LOUIS CARDINALS

BOB MILLER PITCHER
ST. LOUIS CARDINALS

STAN MUSIAL FIRST BASE
ST. LOUIS CARDINALS

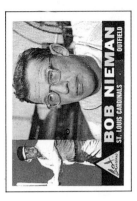
BOB NIEMAN OUTFIELD
ST. LOUIS CARDINALS

GENE OLIVER OUTFIELD-CATCHER
ST. LOUIS CARDINALS

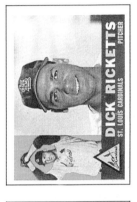
DICK RICKETTS PITCHER
ST. LOUIS CARDINALS

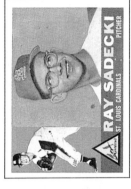
RAY SADECKI PITCHER
ST. LOUIS CARDINALS

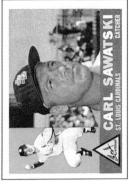
CARL SAWATSKI CATCHER
ST. LOUIS CARDINALS

HAL SMITH CATCHER
ST. LOUIS CARDINALS

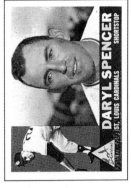
DARYL SPENCER SHORTSTOP
ST. LOUIS CARDINALS

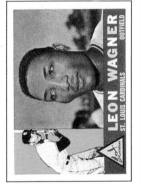
LEON WAGNER OUTFIELD
ST. LOUIS CARDINALS

BILL WHITE OUTFIELD-1st BASE
ST. LOUIS CARDINALS

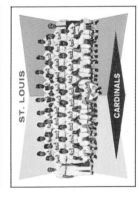
ST. LOUIS CARDINALS

KEANE POLLET
KATT WALKER
ST. LOUIS CARDS COACHES

1961

A pitching breakdown that began in spring training prevented the Cardinals from contending in the 1961 pennant race. League leaders in April, the Birds toppled after that and finally settled in fifth place. Coach Johnny Keane replaced Solly Hemus as manager on July 6 but the shift brought little improvement in the standings. Ken Boyer, with a .329 average and 24 homers, was the Redbirds' top bat. Bill White batted .286 with 20 homers while Stan Musial hit .288 with 15 four-baggers. A heart ailment forced catcher Hal Smith to terminate his career in June. Larry Jackson, suffering a broken jaw in spring training, had a 14-11 record. Ray Sadecki went 14-10 and Curt Simmons 9-10. Bob Gibson was 13-10 and Lindy McDaniel 10-6. Ernie Broglio, a 21-game winner in 1960, slid to 9-12.

KEN BOYER
Third Base

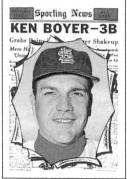
Sporting News
KEN BOYER–3B

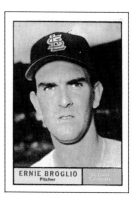
ERNIE BROGLIO
Pitcher

CHRIS CANNIZZARO
Catcher

AL CICOTTE
Pitcher

GEORGE CROWE
First Base

JOE CUNNINGHAM
Outfield

CURT FLOOD
Outfield

BOB GIBSON
Pitcher

ALEX GRAMMAS
Second Base-Shortstop
St. Louis Cardinals

SOLLY HEMUS
Mgr.   St. Louis Cardinals

LARRY JACKSON
Pitcher
St. Louis Cardinals

1961 ROOKIE

CHARLEY JAMES
Outfield
St. Louis Cardinals

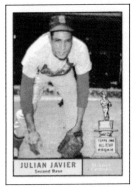

JULIAN JAVIER
Second Base
St. Louis Cardinals

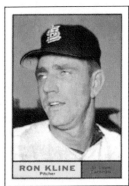

RON KLINE
Pitcher
St. Louis Cardinals

1961 ROOKIE

DON LANDRUM
Outfield

LINDY McDANIEL
Pitcher

BOB MILLER
Pitcher
St. Louis Cardinals

WALT MORYN
Outfield
St. Louis Cardinals

STAN MUSIAL
Outfield

BOB NIEMAN
Outfield

GENE OLIVER
Catcher-Infield-Outfield

RAY SADECKI
Pitcher
St. Louis Cardinals

CARL SAWATSKI
Catcher
St. Louis Cardinals

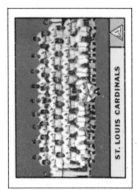

1962

The Cardinals, despite a fast start and a fast finish, slid into sixth place in 1962. The year the National League expanded from eight to 10 clubs didn't benefit manager Johnny Keane's team, which was never really in the hunt following the first month's play. Minnie Minoso, acquired from the White Sox, was limited to 39 games because of a broken wrist, fractured skull and broken left arm. Bill White hit .324 and drove in 102 runs while a rejuvenated Stan Musial batted .330 with 19 homers and 82 RBIs. Ken Boyer batted .291 with two dozen homers and 98 runs batted in. Bob Gibson, 15-13, was one of the top winners among the pitchers. Ernie Broglio was 12-9 and Larry Jackson 16-11. Ray Sadecki went 6-8 and Lindy McDaniel 3-10. Ray Washburn was a 12-game winner and the veteran Curt Simmons ended 10-10.

JOHN ANDERSON
ST. L. CARDS. P

1962 ROOKIE

ED BAUTA
ST. L. CARDINALS P

KEN BOYER
ST. L. CARDS 3 BASE

The Sporting News
NATIONAL LEAGUE ALL-STAR

KEN BOYER
3rd BASE

ERNIE BROGLIO
ST. L. CARDINALS P

JERRY BUCHEK
ST. L. CARDS SS

BOB DULIBA
ST. L. CARDS PITCHER

DON FERRARESE
ST. L. CARDINALS P

CURT FLOOD
ST. L. CARDINALS OF

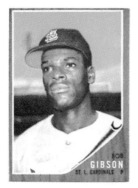

BOB GIBSON
ST. L. CARDINALS P

1962 ROOKIE

JULIO GOTAY
ST. L. CARDS SS

ALEX GRAMMAS
ST. LOUIS CARDS SS

LARRY JACKSON
ST. L. CARDINALS P

CHARLIE JAMES
ST. L. CARDS OF

JULIAN JAVIER
ST. L. CARDS 2 BASE

JOHNNY KEANE
ST. L. CARDS MGR

JOHNNY
KUCKS
ST. LOUIS CARDS P

DON
LANDRUM
ST. L. CARDS OF

TIM
McCARVER
ST. L. CARDS CATCHER

LINDY
McDANIEL
ST. L. CARDINALS P

MINNIE
MINOSO
ST. L. CARDINALS OF

STAN
MUSIAL
ST. L. CARDINALS OF

MUSIAL PLAYS 21ST SEASON

GENE
OLIVER
ST. L. CARDINALS C

RAY
SADECKI
ST. L. CARDS PITCHER

CARL
SAWATSKI
ST. L. CARDINALS C

JIMMY
SCHAFFER
ST. L. CARDINALS C

RED
SCHOENDIENST
ST. L. CARDINALS 2B

CURT
SIMMONS
ST. L. CARDINALS P

BOBBY G.
SMITH
ST. L. CARDINALS OF

CARL
WARWICK
ST. LOUIS CARDS OF

1962 ROOKIE
RAY
WASHBURN
ST. L. CARDINALS P

BILL
WHITE
ST. L. CARDINALS 1B

REDBIRD RIPPERS
LINDY McDANIEL • LARRY JACKSON

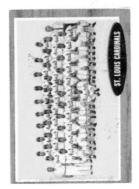
ST. LOUIS CARDINALS

1963

Stan Musial's farewell season almost ended on a winning note, but the Cardinals, contenders from the outset, had to settle for second place, six lengths behind the winning Dodgers in 1963. Musial said goodbye with a .255 batting average and a dozen homers while Ken Boyer hit .285 with 24 homers and 111 RBIs. Shortstop Dick Groat, stabilizing the infield, hit .319. Bill White had 27 homers, 109 RBIs and a .304 average. Curt Flood batted .302 as the Cardinals led the league in hitting with a .271 average. Curt Simmons, 15-9 with a 2.47 ERA, led the Redbirds' pitchers. Bob Gibson won 18 and struck out 204 while Ray Sadecki went 10-10 and Ernie Broglio was 18-8. Ron Taylor won nine games but Ray Washburn, hampered by a bad shoulder, won only five.

GEORGE
ALTMAN
ST. LOUIS CARDINALS OF

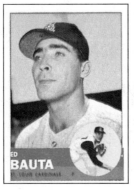
ED
BAUTA
ST. LOUIS CARDINALS P

KEN
BOYER
ST. LOUIS CARDINALS 3B

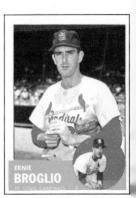
ERNIE
BROGLIO
ST. LOUIS CARDINALS

BOB
DULIBA
ST. LOUIS CARDS   PITCHER

CURT
FLOOD
ST. LOUIS CARDINALS   OF

BOB
GIBSON
ST. LOUIS CARDINALS   P

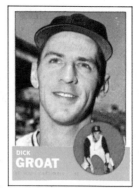

DICK
GROAT

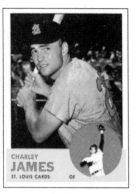

CHARLEY
JAMES
ST. LOUIS CARDS   OF

JULIAN
JAVIER

JOHNNY
KEANE
ST. LOUIS CARDINALS   MGR

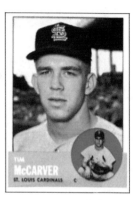

TIM
McCARVER
ST. LOUIS CARDINALS   C

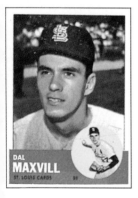

DAL
MAXVILL
ST. LOUIS CARDS   SS

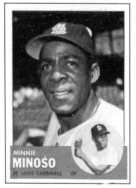

MINNIE
MINOSO
ST. LOUIS CARDINALS   OF

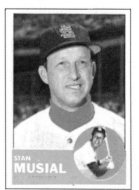

STAN
MUSIAL

GENE
OLIVER

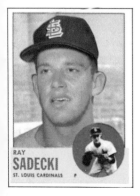

RAY
SADECKI
ST. LOUIS CARDINALS   P

CARL
SAWATSKI
ST. L. CARDINALS   C

BOBBY
SHANTZ
ST. LOUIS CARDS   PITCHER

CURT
SIMMONS
ST. LOUIS CARDS   PITCHER

RAY
WASHBURN
ST. L. CARDS   PITCHER

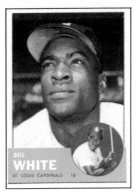

BILL
WHITE
ST. LOUIS CARDINALS   1B

ST. LOUIS CARDINALS

1964

The Cardinals' first National League pennant since 1946 became a reality on the final day of the hectic 1964 season. Rated also-rans on Aug. 24, when they were in fourth place, 11 games behind, the Birds got hot and the Phillies, who led by 7½ with 12 games to go, got cold. It was a four-team scrap for the flag, the Giants being eliminated on the next-to-last day. On the final afternoon the Cardinals beat the Mets, and when the Phillies, who'd lost 10 in a row, downed Cincinnati, it was all over.

A mid-season deal that brought Lou Brock from the Cubs rejuvenated the Cardinals, who won not only the pennant but the World Series from the Yankees in seven games. Brock, batting .348 for the Redbirds, also stole 33 bases. Ken Boyer led the league with 119 RBIs, hit 24 homers and won the MVP award. Bill White hit .303 and had 102 RBIs while Curt Flood hit .311. Bob Gibson, 19-12, wound up the pitching ace though Ray Sadecki won 20 games. Curt Simmons had 18 victories and Ron Taylor, out of the bullpen, won eight. Following the Series win, manager Johnny Keane spurned the Cardinals' offer to renew his contract and instead accepted a deal from the Yankees, whom he'd just defeated.

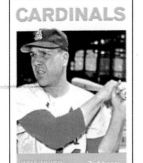

CARDINALS

KEN BOYER   3rd base

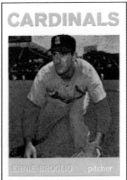

CARDINALS

ERNIE BROGLIO   pitcher

CARDINALS

JERRY BUCHEK   shortstop

CARDINALS

LOU BURDETTE   pitcher

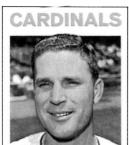

CARDINALS

JIM COKER — catcher

CARDINALS

ROGER CRAIG — pitcher

CARDINALS

CURT FLOOD — outfield

CARDINALS

BOB GIBSON — pitcher

CARDINALS

DICK GROAT — shortstop

CARDINALS

CHARLEY JAMES — outfield

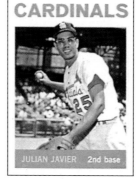

CARDINALS

JULIAN JAVIER — 2nd base

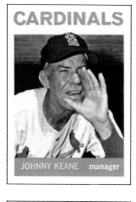

CARDINALS

JOHNNY KEANE — manager

CARDINALS

GARY KOLB — outfield

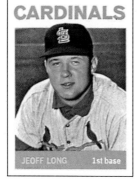

CARDINALS

JEOFF LONG — 1st base

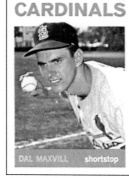

CARDINALS

DAL MAXVILL — shortstop

CARDINALS

TIM McCARVER — catcher

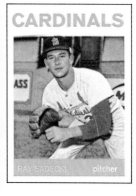

CARDINALS

RAY SADECKI — pitcher

CARDINALS

CARL SAWATSKI — catcher

CARDINALS

BOBBY SHANTZ — pitcher

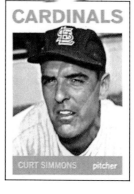

CARDINALS

CURT SIMMONS — pitcher

CARDINALS

RON TAYLOR   pitcher

CARDINALS

BOB UECKER   catcher

CARDINALS

RAY WASHBURN   pitcher

CARDINALS

BILL WHITE   1st base

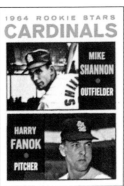

1964 ROOKIE STARS
CARDINALS

MIKE SHANNON
OUTFIELDER

HARRY FANOK
PITCHER

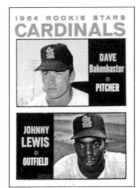

1964 ROOKIE STARS
CARDINALS

DAVE Bakenhaster
PITCHER

JOHNNY LEWIS
OUTFIELD

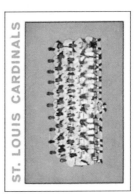

ST. LOUIS CARDINALS

1965

Red Schoendienst made his managerial debut in 1965 and his Cardinals blackjacked him as they skidded all the way to seventh place, the first club to go to such depths while defending the world championship. Injuries and poor relief pitching hurt from the onset. Mike Shannon batted only .221 while bullpenner Barney Schultz was sent back to the minors. Curt Flood led the team with a .310 average. Ken Boyer sagged to .260. Lou Brock hit .288 and Dick Groat .254. Bill White hit .289 with two dozen home runs. Bob Gibson, 20-12, led the Birds' moundsmen. Bob Purkey was 10-9 and Ray Sadecki 6-15. Curt Simmons finished 9-15 while sore-armed Ray Washburn was 9-11 and Tracy Stallard finished 11-8.

CARDS
3rd BASE
KEN BOYER

BOYER'S GRAND-SLAM
GAME #4 ST. LOUIS: 4 NEW YORK: 3
WORLD SERIES

CARDS
OUTFIELD
LOU BROCK

CARDS
SHORTSTOP
JERRY BUCHEK

CARDS
PITCHER
MIKE CUELLAR

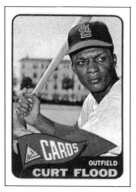

CARDS
OUTFIELD
CURT FLOOD

CARDS
OF-1B
TITO FRANCONA

CARDS
INFIELD
PHIL GAGLIANO

GIBSON WINS FINALE
GAME #7 ST. LOUIS: 7 NEW YORK: 5
WORLD SERIES

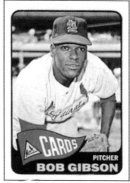

CARDS
PITCHER
BOB GIBSON

CARDS
SHORTSTOP
DICK GROAT

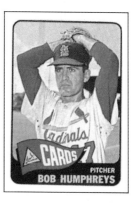

CARDS
PITCHER
BOB HUMPHREYS

CARDS
2nd BASE
JULIAN JAVIER

CARDS
2nd BASE
DAL MAXVILL

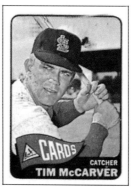

CARDS
CATCHER
TIM McCARVER

CARDS
PITCHER
BOB PURKEY

PITCHER
RAY SADECKI

MANAGER
RED SCHOENDIENST

PITCHER
BARNEY SCHULTZ

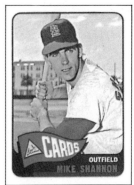

OUTFIELD
MIKE SHANNON

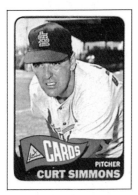

PITCHER
CURT SIMMONS

OUTFIELD
BOB SKINNER

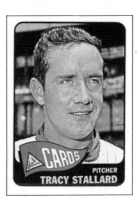

PITCHER
TRACY STALLARD

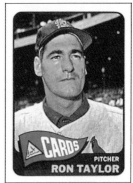

PITCHER
RON TAYLOR

CATCHER
BOB UECKER

OUTFIELD
CARL WARWICK

PITCHER
RAY WASHBURN

1st BASE
BILL WHITE

WORLD SERIES
CARDS TAKE OPENER
GAME #1 ST. LOUIS 9 NEW YORK 5

1965 ROOKIE STARS
outfield BOB TOLAN
pitcher DAVE DOWLING

1965 ROOKIE STARS
infield WAYNE SPIEZIO
pitcher NELSON BRILES

1965 ROOKIE STARS
pitcher STEVE CARLTON
pitcher FRITZ ACKLEY

1966

A weak offense dimmed the Cardinals' flag chances in 1966 and despite the second-best pitching in the league the club finished in sixth place. In June the club moved to its new downtown stadium but the change didn't help in the standings. In May lefthander Ray Sadecki was dealt to the Giants for Orlando Cepeda, who responded with a .301 average plus 20 home runs. Mike Shannon recovered his batting eye to hit .288 with 16 homers. Curt Flood, despite 78 RBIs, hit only .267. Lou Brock led the league with 74 stolen bases and hit .285. Bob Gibson, 21-12, was the staff ace. Lefty Larry Jaster won 11, five of which were shutouts over the flag-winning Dodgers. Al Jackson finished with a 13-15 mark while Ray Washburn turned in an 11-9 effort.

NELSON BRILES pitcher

LOU BROCK outfield

JERRY BUCHEK shortstop

PAT CORRALES catcher

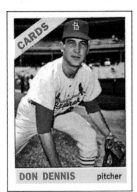

DON DENNIS pitcher

CURT FLOOD outfield

TITO FRANCONA 1b-of

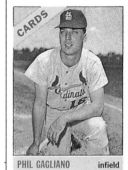

PHIL GAGLIANO infield

BOB GIBSON pitcher

DICK GROAT shortstop

ALVIN JACKSON pitcher

JULIAN JAVIER 2nd base

ART MAHAFFEY pitcher

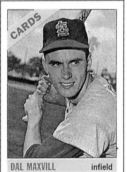

DAL MAXVILL infield

TIM McCARVER catcher

RAY SADECKI pitcher

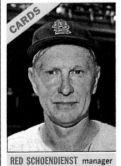

RED SCHOENDIENST manager

MIKE SHANNON outfield

CURT SIMMONS pitcher

BOB SKINNER outfield

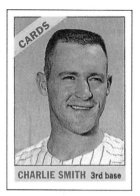

CHARLIE SMITH 3rd base

TRACY STALLARD pitcher

BOB UECKER catcher

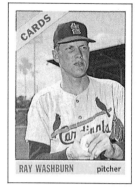

RAY WASHBURN pitcher

HAL WOODESHICK pitcher

1967

Manager Red Schoendienst finally blended pitching with sufficient offense in 1967 and for the Cardinals the result was a runaway National League flag. In addition to winning by 10½, the Redbirds won a seven-game World Series from the Boston Red Sox

Curt Flood's .335 average was tops among the regulars, but Orlando Cepeda, who dubbed the team "El Birdos," was the unanimous MVP winner as he hit .325, hammered 25 homers and led the league with 111 RBIs. Tim McCarver hit a solid .295 while Lou Brock finished at .299 and Roger Maris, acquired from the Yankees, hit .255 with 55 RBIs. Mike Shannon batted just .245 but did drive in 77 runs. Dick Hughes, 16-6, was the Birds' top winner but Bob Gibson was the staff ace. He lost two months because of a leg fracture and still won 13 plus another three in the Series. Nelson Briles, 14-5, and Steve Carlton, 14-9, helped while Ray Washburn won 10 games and Larry Jaster nine.

NELSON BRILES • P

LOU BROCK • OUTFIELD

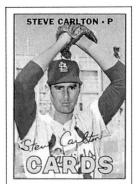

STEVE CARLTON • P

ORLANDO CEPEDA 1B

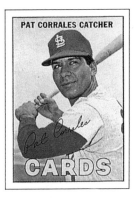

PAT CORRALES CATCHER

CURT FLOOD • OUTFIELD

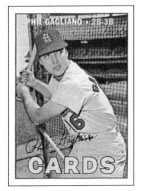

PHIL GAGLIANO • 2B-3B

BOB GIBSON • PITCHER

JOE HOERNER PITCHER

AL JACKSON • PITCHER

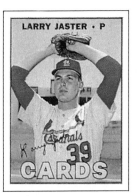

LARRY JASTER • P

JULIAN JAVIER • 2B

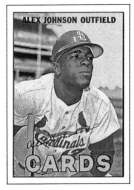

ALEX JOHNSON OUTFIELD

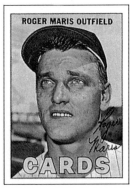

ROGER MARIS OUTFIELD

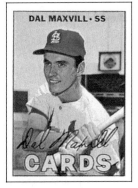

DAL MAXVILL • SS

TIM McCARVER • C

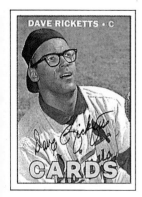

DAVE RICKETTS • C

CARDS

JOHNNY ROMANO • C

CARDS

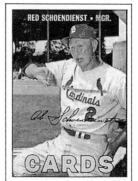

RED SCHOENDIENST • MGR.

CARDS

MIKE SHANNON • 3B-OF

CARDS

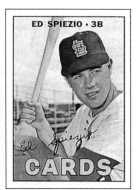

ED SPIEZIO • 3B

CARDS

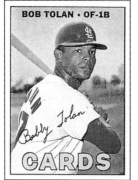

BOB TOLAN • OF-1B

CARDS

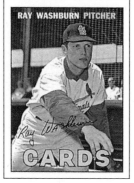

RAY WASHBURN PITCHER

CARDS

HAL WOODESHICK • P

CARDS

LOU BROCK • CURT FLOOD

CARDS CLUBBERS

1967 ROOKIE STARS

DICK HUGHES • P

JIM COSMAN • P

CARDS

CARDS

1968

With magnificent pitching, a sound defense and a so-so offense the Cardinals made it two in a row in 1968, but this time they were defeated, by Detroit, in a seven-game World Series. Bob Gibson, the MVP and Cy Young Award winner, had a superb season. He not only won 22, 13 of them shutouts, but pitched to a 1.12 ERA, the lowest in major league history. His 268 strikeouts were also tops for the league. Nelson Briles won 19 and Ray Washburn 14 while Steve Carlton was 13-11. Curt Flood batted .301 and Lou Brock, despite dipping to a .279 batting mark, led the league in doubles (46), triples (14) and stolen bases (62). Orlando Cepeda hit only .248 and Roger Maris, in his final major league season, batted .255.

JOHN **EDWARDS** — CATCHER · CARDS

CURT **FLOOD** — OUTFIELD · CARDS

PHIL **GAGLIANO** — 2B-SS · CARDS

BOB **GIBSON** — PITCHER · CARDS

GIBSON HURLS SHUTOUT! — WORLD SERIES GAME #4 CARDS: 6 SOX: 0

The Sporting News — ALL STAR SELECTION — BOB GIBSON · PITCHER · NATIONAL LEAGUE

JOE **HOERNER** — PITCHER · CARDS

DICK **HUGHES** — PITCHER · CARDS

LARRY **JASTER** — PITCHER · CARDS

JULIAN **JAVIER** — 2nd BASE · CARDS

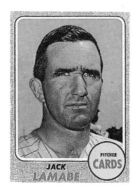

JACK **LAMABE** — PITCHER · CARDS

ROGER **MARIS** — OUTFIELD · CARDS

DAL **MAXVILL** — SHORTSTOP · CARDS

TIM **McCARVER** — CATCHER · CARDS

The Sporting News — ALL STAR SELECTION — TIM McCARVER · CATCHER · NATIONAL LEAGUE

DAVE **RICKETTS** — CATCHER · CARDS

RED
SCHOENDIENST
MANAGER CARDS

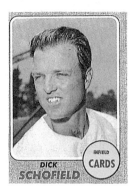

DICK
SCHOFIELD
INFIELD CARDS

MIKE
SHANNON
3rd BASE CARDS

DICK
SIMPSON
OUTFIELD CARDS

ED
SPIEZIO
3rd BASE CARDS

BOB
TOLAN
OUTFIELD CARDS

RAY
WASHBURN
PITCHER CARDS

RON
WILLIS
PITCHER CARDS

1968 ROOKIE STARS
MIKE TORREZ • P
HAL GILSON • P
CARDS

ST. LOUIS WINS IT!
WORLD SERIES GAME #7 CARDS: 7 SOX: 2

THE CARDINALS CELEBRATE!
1967 WORLD SERIES

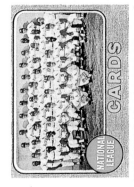

NATIONAL LEAGUE CARDS

1969

The Cardinals' bid for a third straight N.L. pennant in 1969 never got off the ground. Their anemic hitting sank them to fourth place, 13 lengths behind the Miracle Mets as the league embraced divisional play for the first time. Only pitching — their 2.94 ERA was the lowest in the league — kept the Redbirds from sinking even deeper. Bob Gibson won 20 games and Steve Carlton 17. Nelson Briles contributed 15 victories and Mike Torrez 10.

Lou Brock hit .298 and stole 53 bases. Curt Flood batted .285 and Julian Javier .282. Dal Maxvill slumped to .175 while Tim McCarver hit .260. Vada Pinson, bothered by leg ailments, batted .255 with 70 RBIs. Mike Shannon hit only .254 while Joe Torre, obtained from Atlanta for Orlando Cepeda, hit .289 with 18 homers and 101 RBIs.

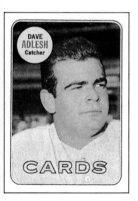
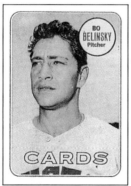
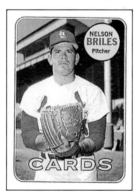
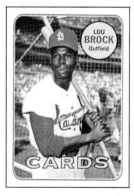

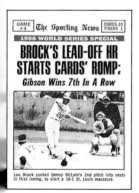
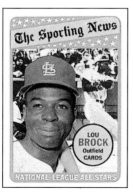
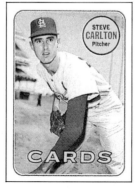

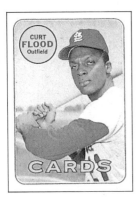

CURT FLOOD
Outfield

CARDS

PHIL GAGLIANO
Infield

CARDS

GAME #1 — The Sporting News — CARDS 4 TIGERS 0

1968 WORLD SERIES SPECIAL

GIBSON FANS 17; SETS NEW RECORD!

Wins 6th Straight Series Game

Bob Gibson yielded only 5 hits as he tamed the Tigers. His 17 strikeouts passed Sandy Koufax' old mark of 15.

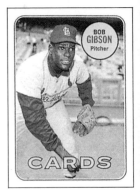

BOB GIBSON
Pitcher

CARDS

The Sporting News

BOB GIBSON
Pitcher
CARDS

NATIONAL LEAGUE ALL-STARS

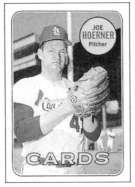

JOE HOERNER
Pitcher

CARDS

DICK HUGHES
Pitcher

CARDS

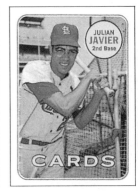

JULIAN JAVIER
2nd Base

CARDS

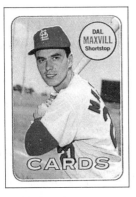

DAL MAXVILL
Shortstop

CARDS

GAME #3 — The Sporting News — CARDS 7 TIGERS 3

1968 WORLD SERIES SPECIAL

McCARVER'S HOMER PUTS ST. LOUIS AHEAD

3-Run Blast Gives Cards Lead

Tim McCarver is greeted by teammates Mike Shannon, Roger Maris and Curt Flood after 5th inning homer.

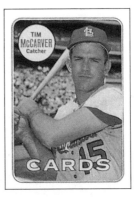

TIM McCARVER
Catcher

CARDS

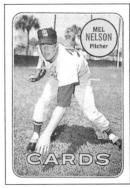

MEL NELSON
Pitcher

CARDS

VADA PINSON
Outfield

CARDS

DAVE RICKETTS
Catcher

CARDS

RED SCHOENDIENST
Manager

CARDS

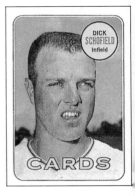

DICK SCHOFIELD
Infield

CARDS

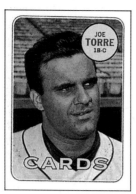
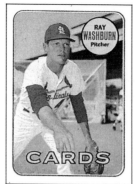
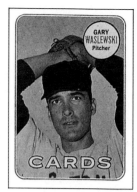
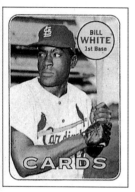
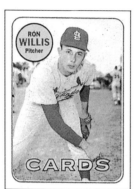

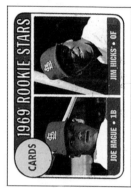

≡1970≡

It was another "down" year for the Cardinals as the pitching, except for 23-game-winner Bob Gibson, the Cy Young Award winner, suffered through the 1970 season. The Redbirds' bullpen, credited with a scant 20 saves, was the chief culprit. Steve Carlton was 10-19 and Nelson Briles 7-6. Mike Torrez finished 8-10 and lefty Jerry Reuss was 7-8. The Birds did come up with some plate punch, however, as Lou Brock batted .304 and had 200 hits for the third straight time. His 51 stolen bases marked the sixth successive season he'd swiped 50 or more. Joe Torre hit .325 with 100 RBIs and Dick Allen, hitting .279, hammered 34 homers and drove in 101 runs. Jose Cardenal contributed with a .293 bat and 74 runs batted in.

Rich Allen | 1ST BASE

Nelson Briles | PITCHER

Lou Brock | OUTFIELD

Jose Cardenal | OUTFIELD

Steve Carlton | PITCHER

George Culver | PITCHER

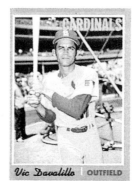
Vic Davalillo | OUTFIELD

Bill Dillman | PITCHER

Phil Gagliano | INFIELD

Bob Gibson | PITCHER

Joe Hague | 1ST BASE

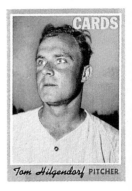
Tom Hilgendorf PITCHER

Steve Huntz | 2B-SS

Julian Javier | 2ND BASE

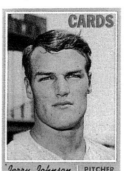
Jerry Johnson | PITCHER

Dal Maxvill | SHORTSTOP

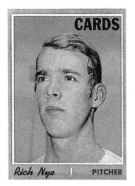

Rich Nye | PITCHER

Cookie Rojas | INFIELD

Red Schoendienst | MGR.

Mike Shannon | 3RD BASE

Carl Taylor | C-OF

Chuck Taylor | PITCHER

Joe Torre | CATCHER-1ST BASE

Mike Torrez | PITCHER

1970 ROOKIE STARS CARDS

SANTIAGO GUZMAN
REGGIE CLEVELAND
SAL CAMPISI

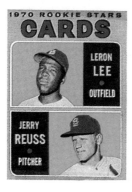

1970 ROOKIE STARS
CARDS

LERON LEE OUTFIELD

JERRY REUSS PITCHER

ST. LOUIS CARDINALS

1971

What was predicted to be another fourth-place windup for the Cardinals instead became a pleasant second-place finish in 1971 as Joe Torre had what's called a career year. Torre, the MVP, led the league with a lusty .363 batting average. In addition he hit 24 homers and led the league with 137 RBIs. Lou Brock batted .313 and led the league with 64 stolen bases. Newcomer Ted Simmons batted .304 and Matty Alou .315. Bob Gibson, despite a tour on the disabled list, won 16 games and Steve Carlton went 20-9. Reggie Cleveland finished 12-12 and Jerry Reuss was 14-14. Reliever Don Shaw won seven and lost two.

CARDS
matty alou · outfield

CARDS
jim beauchamp · outfield

CARDS
frank bertaina · pitcher

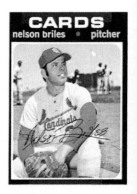
CARDS
nelson briles · pitcher

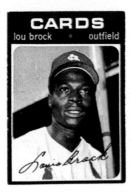
CARDS
lou brock · outfield

CARDS
bob burda · outfield

CARDS
jose cardenal · outfield

CARDS
steve carlton · pitcher

CARDS · ed crosby · shortstop
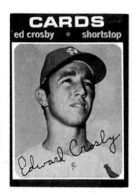

CARDS · jerry da vanon · infield

CARDS · vic davalillo · outfield

CARDS · moe drabowsky · pitcher
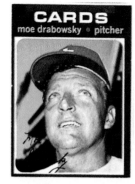

CARDS · bob gibson · pitcher

CARDS · joe hague · 1st base

CARDS · julian javier · 2nd base
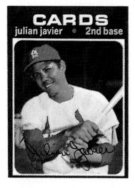

CARDS · leron lee · outfield

CARDS · frank linzy · pitcher
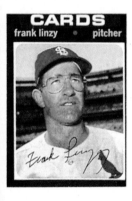

CARDS · dal maxvill · shortstop

CARDS · jerry mc nertney · catcher
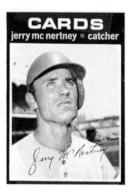

CARDS · fred norman · pitcher
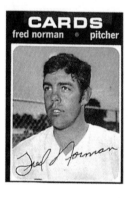

CARDS · milt ramirez · shortstop

CARDS · jerry reuss · pitcher
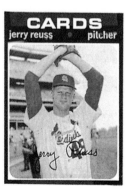

CARDS · red schoendienst · mgr

CARDS · dick schofield · infield
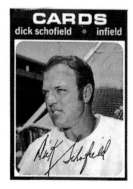

CARDS
mike shannon • 3rd base

CARDS
don shaw • pitcher

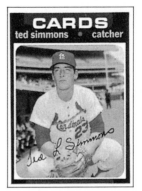

CARDS
ted simmons • catcher

CARDS
ted sizemore • 2b

CARDS
chuck taylor • pitcher

CARDS
joe torre • 3rd base

CARDS
mike torrez • pitcher

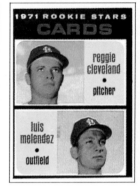

1971 ROOKIE STARS
CARDS
reggie cleveland • pitcher
luis melendez • outfield

1971 ROOKIE STARS
CARDS
AL HRABOSKY
BOB STINSON
BOB CHLUPSA

CARDS

1972

No one expected Joe Torre to repeat his 1971 numbers, but then no one expected the rest of the Cardinals to go into a mass decline in 1972 either. Instead of contending with Pittsburgh for the Eastern Division title, the Redbirds settled for fourth place, 21½ games behind. Lou Brock batted .311 and his 63 stolen bases again led the league. Ted Simmons swung a .303 bat and Matty Alou hit .314. Torre's average dipped to .289 and his 11 homers and 81 RBIs were below his 1971 figures. The trade of Steve Carlton in spring training hurt the Birds' staff. Bob Gibson won 19 but Reggie Cleveland finished with a 14-15 log. Al Santoriini was 8-11. Rick Wise, acquired from Philadelphia for Carlton, finished 16-16.

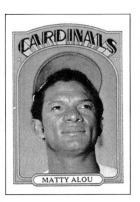
MATTY ALOU

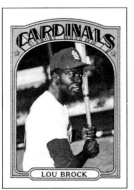
LOU BROCK

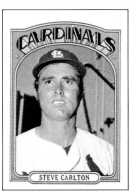
STEVE CARLTON

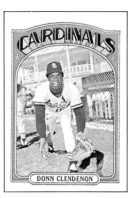
DONN CLENDENON

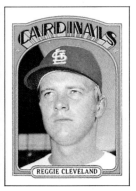
REGGIE CLEVELAND

TONY CLONINGER

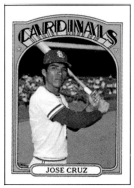
JOSE CRUZ

MOE DRABOWSKY

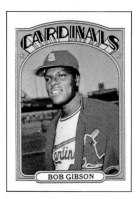

BOB GIBSON

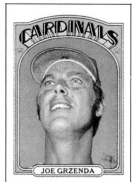

JOE GRZENDA

JOE HAGUE

DENNIS HIGGINS

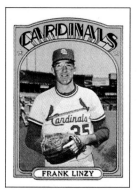

FRANK LINZY

JIM MALONEY

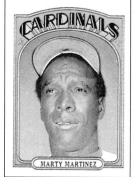

MARTY MARTINEZ

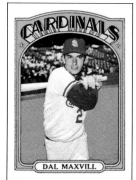

DAL MAXVILL

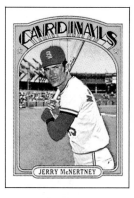

JERRY McNERTNEY

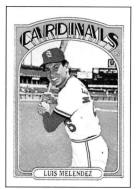

LUIS MELENDEZ

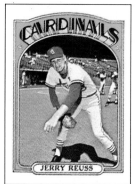

JERRY REUSS

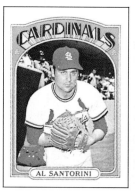

AL SANTORINI

RED SCHOENDIENST

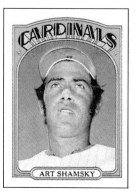

ART SHAMSKY

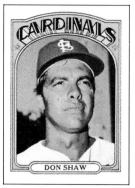

DON SHAW

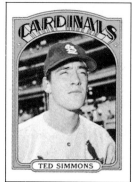

TED SIMMONS

TED SIZEMORE

JOE TORRE

STAN WILLIAMS

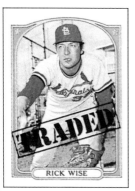

RICK WISE

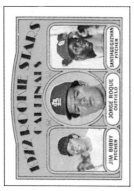

1973

The Cardinals finished second, one and a half lengths behind the division-winning Mets in 1973, but that doesn't tell half the story. The Redbirds opened by losing 12 of 13 and 20 of their first 25. But on Aug. 5, following a long climb, they led the division by five games. However, a September sputter in which they blew one opportunity after another cost them the title.

Bob Gibson, out the first two months with a leg injury, finished with a 12-10 record. Reggie Cleveland was 14-10 and Rick Wise 16-12. A bad shoulder limited Scipio Spinks to a 1-5 season and Alan Foster finished with 13-9. Ted Simmons' .310 average was the best on the offense. Lou Brock hit .297 and stole 70 bases. Jose Cruz, however, batted only .227. Newcomer Bake McBride batted a nice .302 while Joe Torre chipped in with a .287 and 69 runs batted in.

DWAIN
ANDERSON
ST. LOUIS CARDINALS   SHORTSTOP

LOU
BROCK
ST. LOUIS CARDINALS   OUTFIELD

BERNIE
CARBO
ST. LOUIS CARDINALS   OUTFIELD

REGGIE
CLEVELAND
ST. LOUIS CARDINALS   PITCHER

ED
CROSBY
ST. LOUIS CARDINALS   SHORTSTOP

JOSE
CRUZ
ST. LOUIS CARDINALS   OUTFIELD

DON
DURHAM
ST. LOUIS CARDINALS   PITCHER

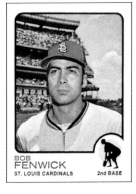

BOB
FENWICK
ST. LOUIS CARDINALS   2nd BASE

RICH
FOLKERS
ST. LOUIS CARDINALS   PITCHER

BOB
GIBSON
ST. LOUIS CARDINALS   PITCHER

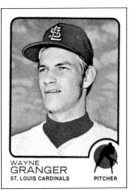

WAYNE
GRANGER
ST. LOUIS CARDINALS   PITCHER

AL
HRABOSKY
ST. LOUIS CARDINALS   PITCHER

TIM
McCARVER
ST. LOUIS CARDINALS   CATCHER

LUIS
MELENDEZ
ST. LOUIS CARDINALS   OUTFIELD

AL
SANTORINI
ST. LOUIS CARDINALS   PITCHER

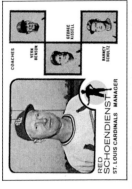

COACHES   VERN BENSON   GEORGE KISSELL   BARNEY SCHULTZ

RED
SCHOENDIENST
ST. LOUIS CARDINALS   MANAGER

DIEGO
SEGUI
ST. LOUIS CARDINALS   PITCHER

TED
SIMMONS
ST. LOUIS CARDINALS   CATCHER

TED
SIZEMORE
ST. LOUIS CARDINALS   2nd BASE

SCIPIO
SPINKS
ST. LOUIS CARDINALS   PITCHER

JOE
TORRE
ST. LOUIS CARDINALS   3rd BASE

RICK
WISE
ST. LOUIS CARDINALS   PITCHER

ST. LOUIS CARDINALS

1974

A solid bullpen and some long-missing batting punch produced a second-place finish for the Cardinals in 1974. Lou Brock set a record with 118 stolen bases and his .306 batting mark gave the Birds a .300-hitting outfield as Rookie of the Year Bake McBride and Reggie Smith each batted .309. Joe Torre, in his final Redbirds season, hit .280 and had 70 runs batted in. Ted Simmons had 103 RBIs and batted .280.

The bullpen, consisting of Al Hrabosky, Mike Garman, Orlando Pena and Rich Folkers, combined for a 26-7 record and 18 saves. Among the starters, Bob Gibson was 11-13 and Lynn McGlothen 16-12. Sonny Siebert ended at 8-8 and Al Foster finished with a 7-10 record.

ST. LOUIS — OUTFIELD
TOMMIE AGEE — CARDINALS

ST. LOUIS — OUTFIELD
LOU BROCK — CARDINALS

ST. LOUIS — PITCHER
REGGIE CLEVELAND — CARDINALS

ST. LOUIS — OUTFIELD
JOSE CRUZ — CARDINALS

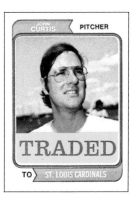

JOHN CURTIS — PITCHER
TRADED
TO — ST. LOUIS CARDINALS

ST. LOUIS — PITCHER
RICH FOLKERS — CARDINALS

ST. LOUIS — PITCHER
ALAN FOSTER — CARDINALS

ST. LOUIS — PITCHER
BOB GIBSON — CARDINALS

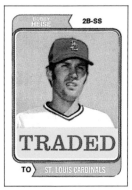

BOBBY HEISE — 2B-SS
TRADED
TO — ST. LOUIS CARDINALS

ST. LOUIS — PITCHER
AL HRABOSKY — CARDINALS

ST. LOUIS — C-1B
TIM McCARVER — CARDINALS

ST. LOUIS — OUTFIELD
LUIS MELENDEZ — CARDINALS

ST. LOUIS — PITCHER
TOM MURPHY — CARDINALS

ST. LOUIS — PITCHER
ORLANDO PENA — CARDINALS

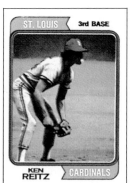

ST. LOUIS — 3rd BASE
KEN REITZ — CARDINALS

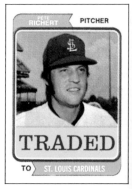

PETE RICHERT — PITCHER
TRADED
TO — ST. LOUIS CARDINALS

ST. LOUIS · MANAGER
· COACHES ·
Barney Schultz · George Kissell · Johnny Lewis · Vern Benson
RED SCHOENDIENST · CARDINALS

ST. LOUIS · PITCHER
DIEGO SEGUI · CARDINALS

ST. LOUIS · PITCHER
SONNY SIEBERT · CARDINALS

ST. LOUIS · CATCHER
TED SIMMONS · CARDINALS

ST. LOUIS · 2nd BASE
TED SIZEMORE · CARDINALS

ST. LOUIS · OUTFIELD
REGGIE SMITH · CARDINALS

ST. LOUIS · PITCHER
SCIPIO SPINKS · CARDINALS

ST. LOUIS · 1B—3B
JOE TORRE · CARDINALS

ST. LOUIS · SHORTSTOP
MIKE TYSON · CARDINALS

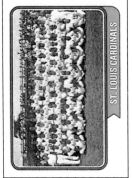

ST. LOUIS CARDINALS

1975

Despite leading the National League with a .273 batting average, the 1974 Cardinals wound up tied for third place with the Mets, 10½ games behind the Pirates. Ted Simmons led the attack with a .332 average that included 18 homers and 100 RBIs. Lou Brock batted .309 and had 56 stolen bases while the newly arrived Willie Davis batted .281. Ron Fairly hit .301 and a young Keith Hernandez batted .250 in 64 games. Bake McBride swung a .300 bat and Ken Reitz batted .269. Reggie Smith weighed in with a .302 plate mark and 76 RBIs. Bob Forsch led the pitchers with 15 wins and John Curtis finished 8-9. Bob Gibson's final Redbirds season saw him end with a 3-10 record. Johnny Denny went 10-7 and Lynn McGlothen was 15-13.

'74 Highlights — BROCK STEALS 118 BASES

CARDINALS — LOU BROCK — Outfield

CARDINALS — JOHN CURTIS — Pitcher

CARDINALS — JIM DWYER — Outfield

CARDINALS — RICH FOLKERS — Pitcher

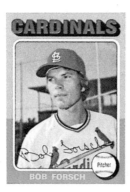

CARDINALS — BOB FORSCH — Pitcher

CARDINALS — ALAN FOSTER — Pitcher

CARDINALS — MIKE GARMAN — Pitcher

'74 Highlights

GIBSON THROWS 3000th STRIKEOUT

CARDINALS

BOB GIBSON

CARDINALS

JACK HEIDEMANN — Shortstop

CARDINALS

AL HRABOSKY — Pitcher

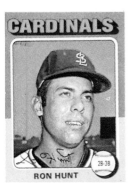

CARDINALS

RON HUNT — 2B-3B

CARDINALS

BAKE McBRIDE — Outfield

CARDINALS

LYNN McGLOTHEN — Pitcher

CARDINALS

LUIS MELENDEZ — Outfield

CARDINALS

CLAUDE OSTEEN — Pitcher

CARDINALS

KEN REITZ — 3rd Base

CARDINALS

KEN RUDOLPH — Catcher

CARDINALS

RAY SADECKI — Pitcher

CARDINALS

SONNY SIEBERT — Pitcher

CARDINALS

TED SIMMONS — Catcher

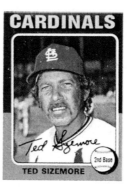

CARDINALS

TED SIZEMORE — 2nd Base

CARDINALS

REGGIE SMITH — Outfield

ELIAS SOSA

CARDINALS

MIKE TYSON

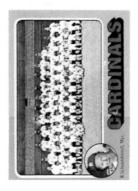

CARDINALS

1976

A weak defense, injuries to key personnel and spotty pitching pushed the 1976 Cardinals into fifth place in the National League East. The season marked Red Schoendienst's final one as manager, a post he'd held since 1965. Bake McBride, riddled by injuries, did hit .335 in 72 games. Reggie Smith, also hurt frequently, batted .218 before being dealt to the Dodgers. Ted Simmons' plate mark slipped to .291 but Lou Brock hit .301 and swiped 56 bases. Keith Hernandez, off to a slow start, finished at .289. John Denny, the league's ERA leader with 2.52, won 11 games. Lynn McGlothen was 13-15 and Bob Forsch 8-10. John Curtis finished 6-11 and Eric Rasmussen 6-12. Pete Falcone, obtained from the Giants, was 12-16.

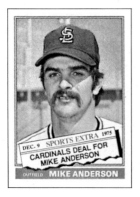

DEC. 9 SPORTS EXTRA 1975
CARDINALS DEAL FOR MIKE ANDERSON
OUTFIELD MIKE ANDERSON

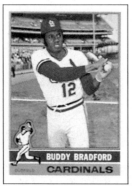

BUDDY BRADFORD
OUTFIELD CARDINALS

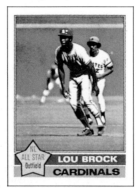

NL ALL STAR Outfield LOU BROCK
CARDINALS

JOHN CURTIS
PITCHER CARDINALS

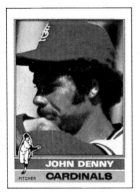

JOHN DENNY
PITCHER CARDINALS

RON FAIRLY
FIRST BASE CARDINALS

DEC. 8 SPORTS EXTRA 1975
LEFTY FALCONE BECOMES
A REDBIRD

PETE FALCONE
PITCHER CARDINALS

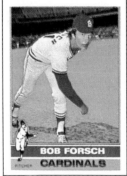

BOB FORSCH
PITCHER CARDINALS

MARIO GUERRERO
THIRD BASE CARDINALS

KEITH HERNANDEZ
FIRST BASE CARDINALS

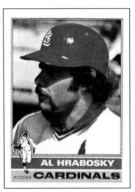

AL HRABOSKY
PITCHER CARDINALS

DON KESSINGER
SHORTSTOP CARDINALS

BAKE McBRIDE
OUTFIELD CARDINALS

LYNN McGLOTHEN
PITCHER CARDINALS

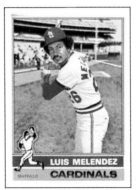

LUIS MELENDEZ
OUTFIELD CARDINALS

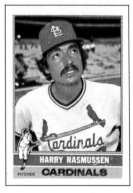

HARRY RASMUSSEN
PITCHER CARDINALS

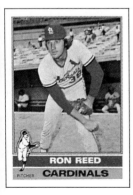

RON REED
PITCHER CARDINALS

KEN REITZ
THIRD BASE CARDINALS

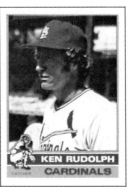

KEN RUDOLPH
CATCHER CARDINALS

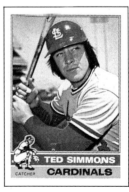

TED SIMMONS
CATCHER CARDINALS

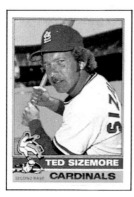
TED SIZEMORE — SECOND BASE — CARDINALS

REGGIE SMITH — OUTFIELD — CARDINALS

MIKE TYSON — SHORTSTOP — CARDINALS

ST. LOUIS CARDINALS

1977

Another late-season collapse doomed the Cardinals' 1977 edition to a third-place windup that left them 18 lengths behind the triumphant Phillies. Vern Rapp's initial season at the Redbirds' helm was one of ups and downs. At various times the hitting and the pitching ran aground. Garry Templeton, in his first full season at shortstop, batted .322. Ted Simmons hit .318 with 21 homers, a club record for a catcher. He had 95 RBIs while Keith Hernandez batted .291 with 17 four-baggers and 79 runs batted in. Among the pitchers, Bob Forsch went 20-7 but John Denny finished 8-8. Pete Falcone was a disappointing 4-8 and Eric Rasmussen finished at 11-17.

CARDINALS — MIKE ANDERSON — OUTFIELD

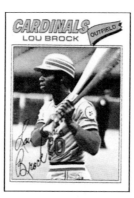
CARDINALS — LOU BROCK — OUTFIELD

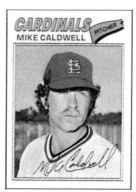
CARDINALS — MIKE CALDWELL — PITCHER

CARDINALS — HECTOR CRUZ — 3rd BASE

CARDINALS PITCHER
JOHN D'ACQUISTO

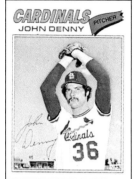

CARDINALS PITCHER
JOHN DENNY

CARDINALS PITCHER
PETE FALCONE

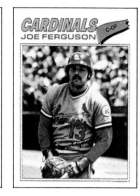

CARDINALS C-OF
JOE FERGUSON

CARDINALS PITCHER
BOB FORSCH

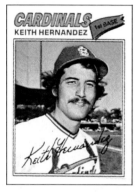

CARDINALS 1st BASE
KEITH HERNANDEZ

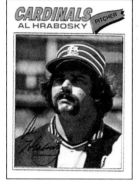

CARDINALS PITCHER
AL HRABOSKY

CARDINALS SS-2B
DON KESSINGER

CARDINALS OUTFIELD
BAKE McBRIDE

CARDINALS PITCHER
LYNN McGLOTHEN

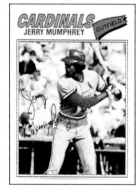

CARDINALS OUTFIELD
JERRY MUMPHREY

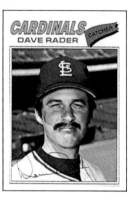

CARDINALS CATCHER
DAVE RADER

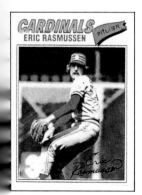

CARDINALS PITCHER
ERIC RASMUSSEN

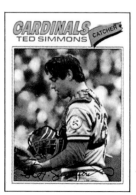

CARDINALS CATCHER
TED SIMMONS

CARDINALS SHORTSTOP
GARRY TEMPLETON

CARDINALS 2nd BASE
MIKE TYSON

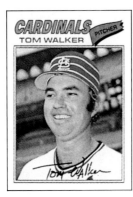

1978

Even an April managerial switch from Vern Rapp to one-time Redbirds' star Ken Boyer failed to right the Cardinals' wrongs in 1978 as the club dipped to fifth place with its worst won-lost record in 54 years.

The team didn't produce a .300 hitter and Ted Simmons' .287 was the best among the regulars. George Hendrick, acquired from the Padres, hit .278. Garry Templeton recovered from a poor start to bat .280. Keith Hernandez slumped to .255 and Ken Reitz, despite 75 RBIs, batted only .246. Bob Forsch, who no-hit the Phillies on April 16, struggled through an 11-17 season. John Denny won 14 and Pete Vukovich went 12-12. Victories by Cardinals lefthanders were virtually non-existent. Their southpaws won a total of four, half of them by Pete Falcone, who finished with a 2-7 record.

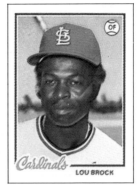

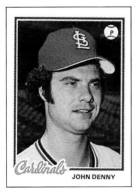

JOHN DENNY

LARRY DIERKER

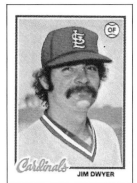

JIM DWYER

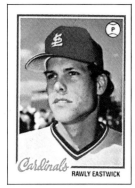

RAWLY EASTWICK

PETE FALCONE

BOB FORSCH

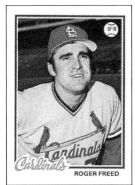

ROGER FREED

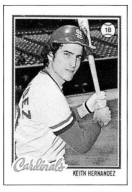

KEITH HERNANDEZ

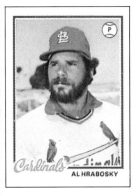

AL HRABOSKY

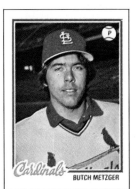

BUTCH METZGER

JERRY MUMPHREY

MIKE PHILLIPS

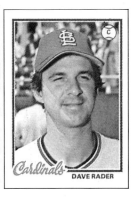

DAVE RADER

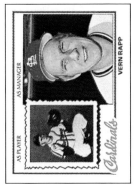

AS PLAYER   AS MANAGER   VERN RAPP

ERIC RASMUSSEN

KEN REITZ

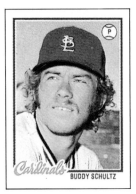
BUDDY SCHULTZ

TONY SCOTT

TED SIMMONS

GARRY TEMPLETON

MIKE TYSON

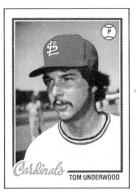
TOM UNDERWOOD

JOHN URREA

≡1979≡

A revitalized Keith Hernandez, whose .344 batting average won the league's batting title and a share of the MVP award with Pittsburgh's Willie Stargell, helped fuel the Cardinals' third-place ending in 1979. Lou Brock's farewell season was a beauty as he collected his 3,000th career hit and set a career record for stolen bases with 938. Brock, who batted .221 in 1978, rebounded to hit .304 in his finale.

Hernandez, hiking his average 89 points, led the majors in doubles (48) and drove in 105 runs. Garry Templeton, despite being unhappy in St.Louis, hit .314. The Redbirds, who led the N.L. with a .278 average, posted five regulars above .300. The pitching, unfortunately, couldn't match the plate production. John Denny finished at 8-11 and soph Silvio Martinez was a 15-game winner. Rookie John Fulgham, pitching half the season, won 10. Pete Vukovich also won 15 while Bob Forsch was 11-11.

LOU BROCK OF
CARDINALS

JOHN DENNY P
CARDINALS

PETE FALCONE P
CARDINALS

BOB FORSCH P
CARDINALS

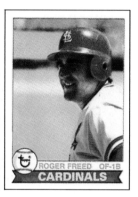
ROGER FREED OF-1B
CARDINALS

WAYNE GARRETT 3B
CARDINALS

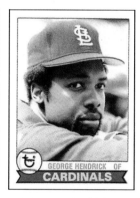
GEORGE HENDRICK OF
CARDINALS

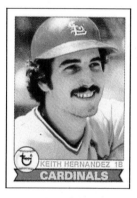
KEITH HERNANDEZ 1B
CARDINALS

MARK LITTELL P
CARDINALS

AURELIO LOPEZ P
CARDINALS

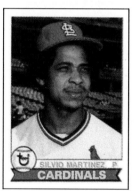
SILVIO MARTINEZ P
CARDINALS

JERRY MORALES OF
CARDINALS

MIKE PHILLIPS 3B-2B
CARDINALS

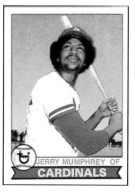
JERRY MUMPHREY OF
CARDINALS

KEN REITZ 3B
CARDINALS

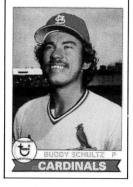
BUDDY SCHULTZ P
CARDINALS

TONY SCOTT OF
CARDINALS

TED SIMMONS C
CARDINALS

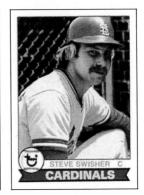
STEVE SWISHER C
CARDINALS

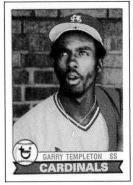
GARRY TEMPLETON SS
CARDINALS

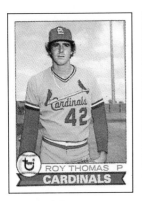
ROY THOMAS P
CARDINALS

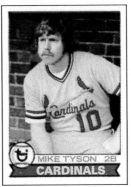
MIKE TYSON 2B
CARDINALS

JOHN URREA P
CARDINALS

PETE VUCKOVICH P
CARDINALS

CARDINALS 1979 PROSPECTS
TERRY KENNEDY CATCHER
GEORGE FRAZIER PITCHER
TOM BRUNO PITCHER

CARDINALS
KEN BOYER MANAGER

1980

Considering the dugout turnover, the Cardinals were fortunate to finish as high as fourth place in the 1980 season. In a year in which they employed 42 players — 21 of them pitchers — the Birds had four managers. Ken Boyer got dumped in June and coach Jack Krol skippered the team for a game. Whitey Herzog took over and in mid-August he was named general manager. Coach Red Schoendienst relieved Herzog in the dugout, but following the season it was announced Herzog would play the manager-general role in 1981. Pete Vukovich (12-9) and Bob Forsch (11-10) were the only pitchers to win more than 10 games. Keith Hernandez hit .321 with 99 RBIs. George Hendrick batted .302 with 25 homers and 109 RBIs. Garry Templeton, missing time because of injuries, hit .318 and Ted Simmons batted .303 with 98 RBIs.

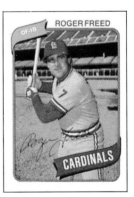

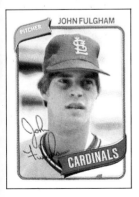

CATCHER — TERRY KENNEDY
CARDINALS

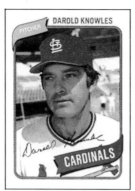

PITCHER — DAROLD KNOWLES
CARDINALS

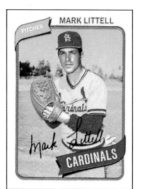

PITCHER — MARK LITTELL
CARDINALS

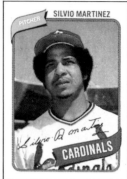

PITCHER — SILVIO MARTINEZ
CARDINALS

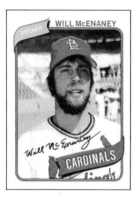

PITCHER — WILL McENANEY
CARDINALS

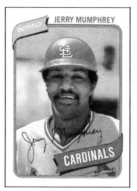

OUTFIELD — JERRY MUMPHREY
CARDINALS

2B-SS — KEN OBERKFELL
CARDINALS

3B-2B — MIKE PHILLIPS
CARDINALS

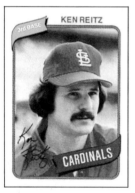

3rd BASE — KEN REITZ
CARDINALS

PITCHER — BUDDY SCHULTZ
CARDINALS

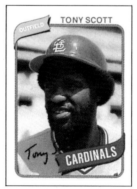

OUTFIELD — TONY SCOTT
CARDINALS

CATCHER — TED SIMMONS
★N.L. ALL-STAR★
CARDINALS

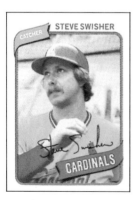

CATCHER — STEVE SWISHER
CARDINALS

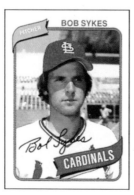

PITCHER — BOB SYKES
CARDINALS

1979 HIGHLIGHTS
Garry Templeton becomes 1st with 100 hits from each side of plate.

SHORTSTOP — GARRY TEMPLETON
CARDINALS

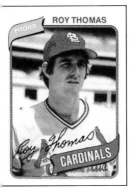

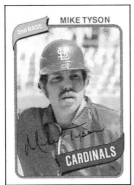

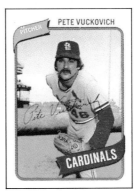

≡1981≡

Despite second-place finishes in both ends of the strike-torn 1981 season, the Cardinals were eliminated from the post-season play that featured a mini-playoff between Montreal and Philadelphia in the N.L. East. George Hendrick's 18 homers and 61 RBIs led the Birds while Keith Hernandez hit .306. Tom Herr batted .268 and Garry Templeton batted .280 after missing games because of medical problems. Darrell Porter, sidelined with a shoulder ailment, hit only .224. Bob Forsch paced Whitey Herzog's pitching corps with 10 wins and Joaquin Andujar, obtained from Houston, won six of seven decisions for the Redbirds. Lefty John Martin was 8-5 but Silvio Martinez, pestered by ailments, won only two games. Bruce Sutter, the relief ace, saved 25 and won the N.L.'s Fireman of the Year prize.

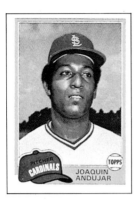

PITCHER
CARDINALS
JOAQUIN
ANDUJAR
TOPPS

OUTFIELD
CARDINALS
BOBBY
BONDS
TOPPS

OUTFIELD
CARDINALS
LEON
DURHAM
TOPPS

PITCHER
CARDINALS
BOB
FORSCH
TOPPS

PITCHER
CARDINALS
JOHN
FULGHAM
TOPPS

OUTFIELD
CARDINALS
GEORGE
HENDRICK
TOPPS

1st BASE
CARDINALS
KEITH
HERNANDEZ
TOPPS

SHORTSTOP
CARDINALS
TOM
HERR
TOPPS

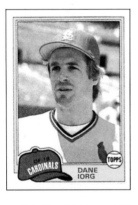

OF-1B
CARDINALS
DANE
IORG
TOPPS

PITCHER
CARDINALS
JIM
KAAT
TOPPS

C-OF
CARDINALS
TERRY
KENNEDY
TOPPS

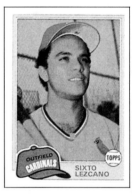

OUTFIELD
CARDINALS
SIXTO
LEZCANO
TOPPS

PITCHER
CARDINALS
MARK
LITTELL
TOPPS

PITCHER
CARDINALS
JOHN
LITTLEFIELD
TOPPS

PITCHER
CARDINALS
SILVIO
MARTINEZ
TOPPS

2nd BASE
CARDINALS
KEN
OBERKFELL
TOPPS

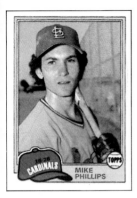

MIKE
PHILLIPS
CARDINALS

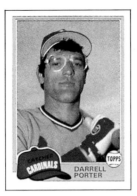

DARRELL
PORTER
CARDINALS

MIKE
RAMSEY
CARDINALS

KEN
REITZ
CARDINALS

TONY
SCOTT
CARDINALS

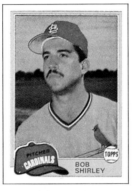

BOB
SHIRLEY
CARDINALS

TED
SIMMONS
CARDINALS

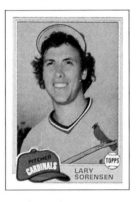

LARY
SORENSEN
CARDINALS

BRUCE
SUTTER
CARDINALS

STEVE
SWISHER
CARDINALS

BOB
SYKES
CARDINALS

GARRY
TEMPLETON
CARDINALS

GENE
TENACE
CARDINALS

JOHN
URREA
CARDINALS

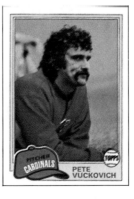

PETE
VUCKOVICH
CARDINALS

CARDINALS FUTURE STARS
ANDY RINCON PITCHER
AL OLMSTED PITCHER
TITO LANDRUM OUTFIELD
TOPPS

1982

Consistency was the word to describe the Cardinals in 1982, a season in which they won it all, including a seventh-game World Series win over Milwaukee. For instance, Whitey Herzog's club didn't lose more than three in a row until after they'd clinched the divisional crown in September.

Ozzie Smith, acquired from San Diego for Garry Templeton, was a superb shortstop and newcomer Lonnie Smith (.307) and Willie McGee (.296) complemented Smith. Tom Herr hit .266 and George Hendrick led the team with 19 homers and 104 RBIs. Keith Hernandez batted .299. Joaquin Andujar was a 15-game winner, as was Bob Forsch. Rookie John Stuper and Dave LaPoint each won nine. Doug Bair and Bruce Sutter handled the bullpen duties, with the latter winning nine and having a major league high of 36 saves.

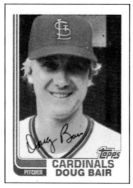

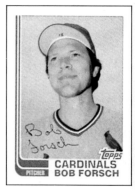

CARDINALS
SS-2B JULIO GONZALEZ

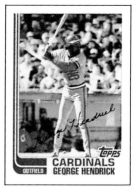

CARDINALS
OUTFIELD GEORGE HENDRICK

CARDINALS
1st BASE KEITH HERNANDEZ

CARDINALS
3rd BASE TOM HERR

CARDINALS
OF-1B DANE IORG

CARDINALS
PITCHER JIM KAAT

CARDINALS
OUTFIELD TITO LANDRUM

CARDINALS
OUTFIELD SIXTO LEZCANO

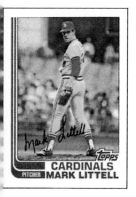

CARDINALS
PITCHER MARK LITTELL

CARDINALS
PITCHER JOHN MARTIN

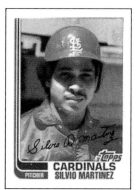

CARDINALS
PITCHER SILVIO MARTINEZ

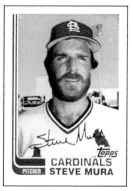

CARDINALS
PITCHER STEVE MURA

CARDINALS
2nd BASE KEN OBERKFELL

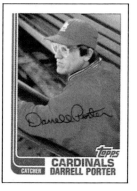

CARDINALS
CATCHER DARRELL PORTER

DARRELL PORTER
in action

CARDINALS
SS-2B MIKE RAMSEY

CARDINALS
PITCHER ANDY RINCON

CARDINALS
CATCHER ORLANDO SANCHEZ

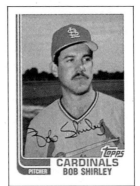

CARDINALS
PITCHER BOB SHIRLEY

CARDINALS
OUTFIELD LONNIE SMITH

CARDINALS
SHORTSTOP OZZIE SMITH

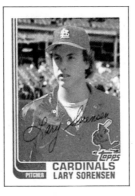

CARDINALS
PITCHER LARY SORENSEN

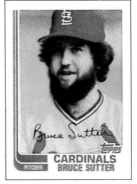

CARDINALS
PITCHER BRUCE SUTTER

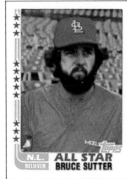

ALL STAR
N.L. RELIEVER BRUCE SUTTER

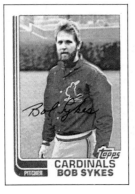

CARDINALS
PITCHER BOB SYKES

CARDINALS
SHORTSTOP GARRY TEMPLETON

CARDINALS
CATCHER GENE TENACE

ST. LOUIS CARDINALS
'81 BATTING & PITCHING LDRS.

ST. LOUIS CARDINALS
FUTURE STARS

1983

The Cardinals' reign as world champions didn't last long as the club, lacking consistent pitching and needing hitting, dropped to fourth place, four games below .500, in 1983. Keith Hernandez was traded to the Mets in June and his offensive contributions were missed. George Hendrick batted .318 with 18 homers and 97 RBIs. David Green batted .284 with 69 RBIs. Darrell Porter hit .262 while Willie McGee finished at .286. Whitey Herzog's pitching wasn't up to par as Dave LaPoint, John Stuper and Neil Allen (acquired for Hernandez) each won a dozen. Bob Forsch, who no-hit Montreal in September, finished 10-12. Bruce Sutter, the bullpen star, was 9-10 with 21 saves.

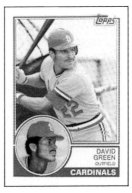

GEORGE
HENDRICK
OUTFIELD
CARDINALS

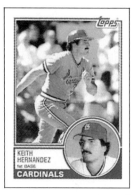

KEITH
HERNANDEZ
1st BASE
CARDINALS

TOM
HERR
2nd BASE
CARDINALS

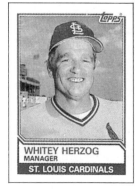

WHITEY HERZOG
MANAGER
ST. LOUIS CARDINALS

DANE
IORG
OUTFIELD-1st BASE
CARDINALS

JIM
KAAT
PITCHER
CARDINALS

* SUPER VETERAN * JIM KAAT
1983
1959

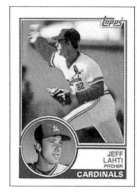

JEFF
LAHTI
PITCHER
CARDINALS

TITO
LANDRUM
OUTFIELD
CARDINALS

DAVE
LaPOINT
PITCHER
CARDINALS

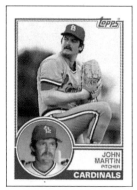

JOHN
MARTIN
PITCHER
CARDINALS

WILLIE
McGEE
OUTFIELD
CARDINALS

STEVE
MURA
PITCHER
CARDINALS

KEN
OBERKFELL
3rd BASE
CARDINALS

DARRELL
PORTER
CATCHER
CARDINALS

JAMIE
QUIRK
C-3B
CARDINALS

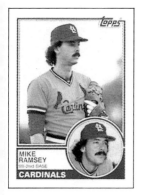

MIKE RAMSEY
SS-2nd BASE
CARDINALS

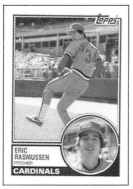

ERIC RASMUSSEN
PITCHER
CARDINALS

LONNIE SMITH
OUTFIELD
CARDINALS

OZZIE SMITH
SHORTSTOP
CARDINALS

JOHN STUPER
PITCHER
CARDINALS

BRUCE SUTTER
PITCHER
CARDINALS

BRUCE SUTTER
PITCHER
ALL STAR
N L

GENE TENACE
CATCHER-1st BASE
CARDINALS

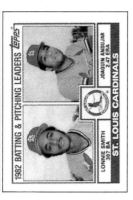

1982 BATTING & PITCHING LEADERS
JOAQUIN ANDUJAR
2.47 ERA
LONNIE SMITH
.307 BA
ST. LOUIS CARDINALS

1984

A strong September enabled the Cardinals to wind up in third place in the National League East in 1984. A paltry offense hurt the Redbirds. Willie McGee's .291 was the club's highest batting average. David Green hit .268 and George Hendrick .277. Barrell Porter struggled at .232 and Ozzie Smith hit .277. Lonnie Smith's best was .250. Newcomer Andy Van Slyke hit .244 while another rookie, Terry Pendleton, playing 67 games, hit .324. A back injury restricted Bob Forsch's pitching and he was 2-5. Joaquin Andujar was 20-14 and lefty Dave LaPoint won a dozen. Kurt Kepshire was 6-5 and Rick Horton went 9-4. Neil Allen was 9-6 and Bruce Sutter won five and saved 45 more.

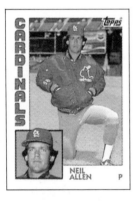
NEIL ALLEN   P

JOAQUIN ANDUJAR   P

STEVE BRAUN   3B-OF

GLENN BRUMMER   C

KEN DAYLEY   P

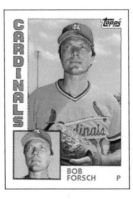
BOB FORSCH   P

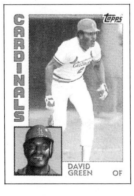
DAVID GREEN   OF

KEVIN HAGEN   P

GEORGE HENDRICK 1B

GEORGE HENDRICK 1B

TOM HERR 2B

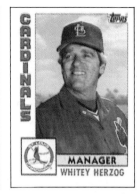
MANAGER WHITEY HERZOG

RICKY HORTON P

ART HOWE 3B

DANE IORG OF-1B

MIKE JORGENSEN OF-1B

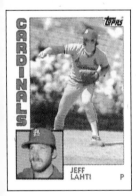
JEFF LAHTI P

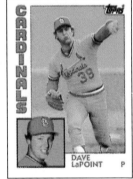
DAVE LaPOINT P

WILLIE McGEE OF

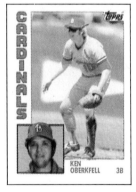
KEN OBERKFELL 3B

DARRELL PORTER C

JAMIE QUIRK C-3B

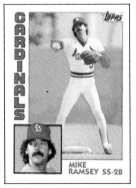
MIKE RAMSEY SS-2B

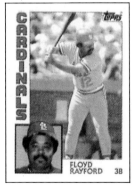
FLOYD RAYFORD 3B

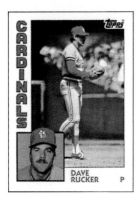

CARDINALS

DAVE
RUCKER P

CARDINALS

LONNIE
SMITH OF

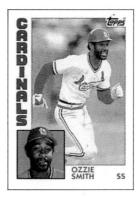

CARDINALS

OZZIE
SMITH SS

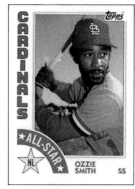

CARDINALS

ALL-STAR
NL

OZZIE
SMITH SS

CARDINALS

JOHN
STUPER P

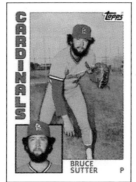

CARDINALS

BRUCE
SUTTER P

CARDINALS

ANDY
VAN SLYKE OF-1B

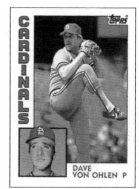

CARDINALS

DAVE
VON OHLEN P

BATTING & PITCHING LEADERS

CARDINALS

JOHN STUPER
3.68 ERA

LONNIE SMITH
.321 BA

≡1985

Pitching, hitting and an amazing 314 stolen bases paved the way for the Cardinals' National League pennant in 1985. However, a seventh-game defeat in the World Series against Kansas City blurred their dream season.

Rookie of the Year outfielder Vince Coleman batted .267 and set a freshman record with 110 stolen bases. Willie McGee, the MVP, was also the batting titlist with a .353 average. Tom Herr hit .302 and Jack Clark, obtained from the Giants, hit 22 homers and drove in 87 runners. Ozzie Smith, in addition to winning his sixth consecutive Gold Glove at shortstop, batted .281. John Tudor, acquired from Pittsburgh, was 21-8, while Joaquin Andujar was 21-12. Danny Cox was an 18-game winner and Kurt Kepshire chalked 10 victories. Bob Forsch won nine. With Bruce Sutter lost to free agency, the Cardinals tried a "bullpen by committee" as Jeff Lahti saved 19, Ken Dayley 11, Bill Campbell four and the late-arriving Todd Worrell going 3-0 with five saves in 21.2 relief innings.

CARDINALS
P
NEIL ALLEN

CARDINALS
P
JOAQUIN ANDUJAR

CARDINALS
3B-OF
STEVE BRAUN

CARDINALS
P
DANNY COX

CARDINALS
P
BOB FORSCH

CARDINALS
1B
DAVID GREEN

CARDINALS
OF
GEORGE HENDRICK

CARDINALS
2B
TOM HERR

CARDINALS
MANAGER
WHITEY HERZOG

CARDINALS
P
RICKY HORTON

CARDINALS
3B-1B
ART HOWE

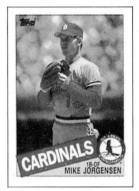

CARDINALS
1B-OF
MIKE JORGENSEN

CARDINALS
P
KURT KEPSHIRE

CARDINALS
P
JEFF LAHTI

CARDINALS
OF
TITO LANDRUM

CARDINALS
P
DAVE LaPOINT

CARDINALS
OF
WILLIE McGEE

CARDINALS
C
TOM NIETO

CARDINALS
3B
TERRY PENDLETON

CARDINALS
C
DARRELL PORTER

CARDINALS
P
DAVE RUCKER

CARDINALS
OF
LONNIE SMITH

CARDINALS
SS
OZZIE SMITH

OZZIE SMITH
SHORTSTOP
ALL STAR
NL

  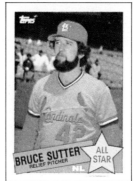 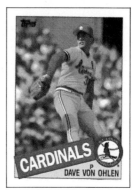

≡1986≡

The Cardinals, as they did in 1983 when they slid from world champions to fourth place, spent the 1986 season slipping from league champions to third place, three games below .500. Their .236 batting average was the lowest in the league and the club's 58 homers were also the fewest in the loop. Willie McGee, the 1985 MVP and league batting champ at .353, couldn't come close to that in 1986 as he hit a lackluster .256. Slugger Jack Clark, limited to 65 games because of an injury, was unable to produce any power. Soph Vince Coleman, despite leading the league with 107 stolen bases, batted a mere .232. The Redbirds' pitching wasn't up to par, either. John Tudor went from 21-8 to 13-7 last year while Bob Forsch was 14-10 and Danny Cox 12-13. Todd Worrell, despite a 9-10 record, was one of the league's premier relievers with 36 saves.

JOAQUIN ANDUJAR

STEVE BRAUN

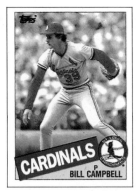
CARDINALS
P
BILL CAMPBELL

BILL CAMPBELL

CESAR CEDENO

CARDINALS
1B
JACK CLARK

1B
JACK CLARK

CARDINALS
OF
VINCE COLEMAN

'85 RECORD BREAKER
VINCE COLEMAN, ST. LOUIS CARDINALS
Most Stolen Bases, Season, Rookie

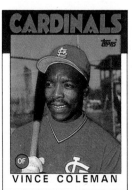
CARDINALS
OF
VINCE COLEMAN

CARDINALS
P
DANNY COX

CARDINALS
P
KEN DAYLEY

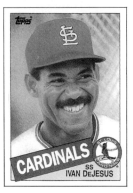
CARDINALS
SS
IVAN DeJESUS

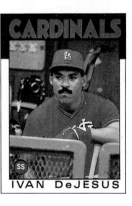
CARDINALS
SS
IVAN DeJESUS

CARDINALS
P
BOB FORSCH

CARDINALS
OF
BRIAN HARPER

CARDINALS

TOM HERR

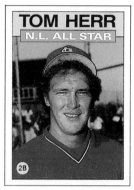

TOM HERR
N.L. ALL STAR

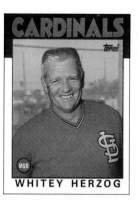

CARDINALS

WHITEY HERZOG

CARDINALS

RICKY HORTON

CARDINALS

RANDY HUNT

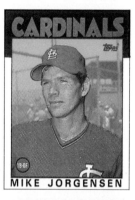

CARDINALS

MIKE JORGENSEN

CARDINALS

KURT KEPSHIRE

CARDINALS

JEFF LAHTI

CARDINALS

TITO LANDRUM

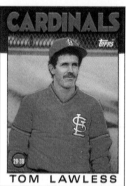

CARDINALS

TOM LAWLESS

CARDINALS

WILLIE McGEE

WILLIE McGEE
N.L. ALL STAR

CARDINALS

TOM NIETO

CARDINALS

TERRY PENDLETON

CARDINALS

DARRELL PORTER

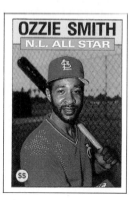

OZZIE SMITH
N.L. ALL STAR

OZZIE SMITH

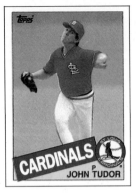

CARDINALS
JOHN TUDOR

JOHN TUDOR

JOHN TUDOR
N.L. ALL STAR

ANDY VAN SLYKE

CARDINALS LEADERS

1987

Despite having many days when it seemed there were more names on the disabled list than the roster, the Cardinals' 1987 season went all the way to the seventh game of the World Series.

Their efforts earned Whitey Herzog further managerial laurels, but there were too many times his injury-dotted club had him wondering if they could finish the schedule. Jack Clark sat out the League Championship Series and World Series and pitching ace John Tudor, victim of a freak broken leg, didn't pitch competitively until late August.

Clark, with 86 RBIs in the first half of the season, was afflicted by a series of injuries and finished with 35 homers and 106 RBIs, one more than outfielder Willie McGee drove in. Ozzie Smith, whose .303 average led the Redbirds' regulars, had 75 RBIs without benefit of a single home run. The Cardinals' ninety four homers were the fewest in the majors.

As usual, the Cardinals' base stealing made the difference. Vince Coleman led both leagues with 109 as Herzog's "rabbits" swiped 248 stolen sacks. The pitching wasn't spectacular, but Herzog, with his deft touch, got amazing mileage from his staff.

Danny Cox, Bob Forsch and Greg Mathews each won 11, while Tudor, working in 16 games and 96 innings, was 10-2. Rookie lefty Joe Magrane was 9-7 and fellow southpaw Ricky Horton went 8-3. Ken Dayley and Todd Worrell provided bullpen help. Dayley went 9-5 with a 2.58 ERA and four saves, while his hard-throwing playmate was 8-6 with 33 saves and a 2.66 earned run average.

JACK CLARK

VINCE COLEMAN

TIM CONROY

DANNY COX

KEN DAYLEY

CURT FORD

BOB FORSCH

TOM HERR

WHITEY HERZOG

RICKY HORTON

CLINT HURDLE

MIKE LAGA

JEFF LAHTI

STEVE LAKE

TITO LANDRUM

MIKE LaVALLIERE

TOM LAWLESS

JIM LINDEMAN

JOE MAGRANE

GREG MATHEWS

WILLIE McGEE

JOHN MORRIS

JOSE OQUENDO

TONY PENA

TERRY PENDLETON

PAT PERRY

OZZIE SMITH

OZZIE SMITH

ALL STAR

RAY SOFF

JOHN TUDOR

ANDY VAN SLYKE

TODD WORRELL

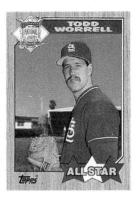

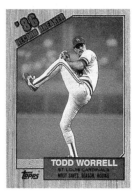

1988

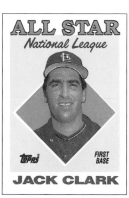

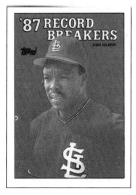

KEN DAVLEY

CURT FORD

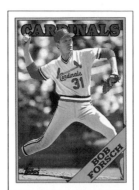
BOB FORSCH

TOM HERR

WHITEY HERZOG
Manager

RICKY HORTON

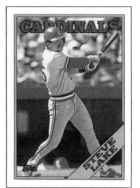
STEVE LAKE

TOM LAWLESS

JIM LINDEMAN

WILLIE McGEE

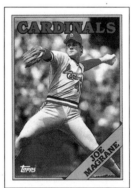
JOE MAGRANE

GREG MATHEWS

JOHN MORRIS

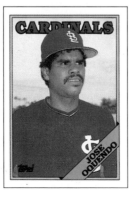
JOSE OQUENDO

TOM PAGNOZZI

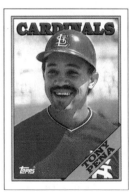
TONY PENA

ALL STAR
National League

Topps   SHORTSTOP

OZZIE SMITH

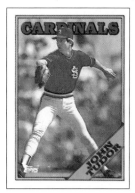

CARDINALS

BOB GIBSON

Universally recognized by both teammates and opponents as perhaps baseball's most intense competitor of his day, Bob Gibson was accorded the honor of being the most dominant pitcher of the 1960s.

In his 17 seasons with the Cardinals, the hard-throwing right-hander posted some awesome numbers. Five times a 20-game winner, 56 of his 251 career wins were shutouts. In 1968 he pitched to a microscopic 1.12 ERA, the lowest ever by a hurler working 300 or more innings. While pitching 13 shutouts and winning 15 straight that season, Gibson had a stretch of 48 scoreless innings and allowed only two runs in 90 frames.

One of the game's top strikeout artists, Bob fanned 3,117 batters and in nine of his seasons exceeded 200 K's. From 1968 to 1971, when he won 65 games, Gibson fanned 811 batters in 912.2 innings.

Winner of seven World Series games, including three over Boston in 1967, Gibson pitched to a 1.89 ERA and fanned 92 in 81 post-season innings. Following the required five-year wait, Gibson gained Hall of Fame honors in 1981.

LOU BROCK OF
CARDINALS

Baseball's all-time stolen-base leader with 938 thefts in his 19 major league seasons, Lou Brock, a .293 lifetime hitter, eight times led the National League in stolen bases.

Initially employed by the Chicago Cubs, Brock was traded to St. Louis in June 1964 and his career took off from there. The deal turned Brock from a good player into a great one. From 1965 through 1976 the outfielder stole 50 or more bases a record 12 times. In 1974 he swiped a then major league record of 118.

In three of his first five seasons in St. Louis, Brock performed for pennant winners. He batted a composite .391 and in 1967 and 1968 stole a record seven bases in each World Series.

Lou, who collected his 3,000th base hit in 1979, his final major league season, became eligible for the Hall of Fame in 1985 and gained his Cooperstown recognition on his maiden try.

If he isn't the finest player in Cardinals history, then Stan Musial is certainly the most popular. Even today, 25 years after collecting his 3,630th and final major league base hit, Stan the Man remains Mr. Baseball in St. Louis.

A .331 lifetime hitter, with 475 home runs and 1,951 RBIs during his 22-season career, Musial, a vice president and member of the Cardinals' board of directors, remains a fan favorite.

Six times the National League's batting champion, Musial appeared in 24 All Star Games and his six homers remains the record for such contests. On three occasions he was voted the coveted Most Valuable Player award.

One of very few to appear in 1,000 or more games at two positions — outfielder and first base — the easygoing, affable Musial, who hit .300 or better for 17 straight seasons, was elected to the Hall of Fame when he appeared on 93% of the ballots in 1969, his first year of Cooperstown eligibility.

1951: Blue Back of Johnny Mize (50) lists for $25 . . . Red Back of Duke Snider (38) lists for $18 . . . Complete set of 9 Team Cards lists for $900 . . . Complete set of 11 Connie Mack All-Stars lists for $2750 with Babe Ruth and Lou Gehrig listing for $700 each . . . Current All-Stars of Jim Konstanty, Robin Roberts and Eddie Stanky list for $4000 each . . . Complete set lists for $14,250.

1952: Mickey Mantle (311) is unquestionably the most sought-after post-war gum card, reportedly valued at $6,500-plus . . . Ben Chapman (391) is photo of Sam Chapman . . . Complete set lists in excess of $36,000.

1953: Mickey Mantle (82) and Willie Mays (244) list for $1,500 each . . . Set features first TOPPS card of Hall-of-Famer Whitey Ford (207) and only TOPPS card of Hall-of-Famer Satchel Paige (220). Pete Runnels (219) is photo of Don Johnson . . . Complete set lists for $9,500.

1954: Ted Williams is depicted on two cards (1 and 250) . . . Set features rookie cards of Hank Aaron (128), Ernie Banks (94) and Al Kaline (201) . . . Card of Aaron lists for $650 . . . Card of Willie Mays (90) lists for $200 . . . Complete set lists for $5,500.

1955: Set features rookie cards of Sandy Koufax (123), Harmon Killebrew (124) and Roberto Clemente (164) . . . The Clemente and Willie Mays (194) cards list for $425 each . . .Complete set lists for $3,900.

1956: Set features rookie cards of Hall-of-Famers Will Harridge (1), Warren Giles (2), Walter Alston (8) and Luis Aparicio (292) . . . Card of Mickey Mantle (135) lists for $650 . . . Card of Willie Mays (130) lists for $125 . . . Complete set lists for $4,000 . . . The Team Cards are found both dated (1955) and undated and are valued at $15 (dated) and more . . . There are two unnumbered Checklist Cards valued high.

1957: Set features rookie cards of Don Drysdale (18), Frank Robinson (35) and Brooks Robinson (328) . . . A reversal of photo negative made Hank Aaron (20) appear as a left-handed batter . . . Card of Mickey Mantle (95) lists for $600 . . . Cards of Brooks Robinson and Sandy Koufax (302) list for $275 each . . . Complete set lists for $4,800.

1958: Set features first TOPPS cards of Casey Stengel (475) and Stan Musial (476) . . . Mike McCormick (37) is photo of Ray Monzant . . . Milt Bolling (188) is photo of Lou Berberet . . . Bob Smith (226) is photo of Bobby Gene Smith . . . Card of Mickey Mantle (150) lists for $400 . . . Card of Ted Williams (1) lists for $325 . . . Complete set lists for $4,800.

1959: In a notable error, Lou Burdette (440) is shown posing as a left-handed pitcher . . . Set features rookie card of Bob Gibson (514) . . . Ralph Lumenti (316) is photo of Camilo Pascual . . . Card of Gibson lists for $200 . . . Card of Mickey Mantle (10) lists for $300 . . . Complete set lists for $3,000.

1960: A run of 32 consecutively numbered rookie cards (117-148) includes the first card of Carl Yastrzemski (148) . . . J.C. Martin (346) is photo of Gary Peters . . . Gary Peters (407) is photo of J.C. Martin . . . Card of Yastrzemski lists for $150 . . . Card of Mickey Mantle (350) lists for $300 . . . Complete set lists for $2,600.

1961: The Warren Spahn All-Star (589) should have been numbered 587 . . . Set features rookie cards of Billy Williams (141) and Juan Marichal (417) . . . Dutch Dotterer (332) is photo of his brother, Tommy . . . Card of Mickey Mantle (300) lists for $200 . . . Card of Carl Yastrzemski (287) lists for $90 . . . Complete set lists for $3,600.

1962: Set includes special Babe Ruth feature (135-144) . . . some Hal Reniff cards numbered 139 should be 159 . . . Set features rookie card of Lou Brock (387) . . . Gene Freese (205) is shown posing as a left-handed batter . . . Card of Mickey Mantle (200) lists for $325 . . . Card of Carl Yastrzemski (425) lists for $125 . . . Complete set lists for $3,300.

1963: Set features rookie card of Pete Rose (537), which lists for $500-plus . . . Bob Uecker (126) is shown posing as a left-handed batter . . . Don Landrum (113) is photo of Ron Santo . . . Eli Grba (231) is photo of Ryne Duren . . . Card of Mickey Mantle (200) lists for $200 . . . Card of Lou Brock (472) lists for $75 . . . Complete set lists for $2,900.

1964: Set features rookie cards of Richie Allen (243), Tony Conigliaro (287) and Phil Niekro (541) . . . Lou Burdette is again shown posing as a left-handed pitcher . . . Bud Bloomfield (532) is photo of Jay Ward . . . Card of Pete Rose (125) lists for $150 . . . Card of Mickey Mantle (50) lists for $175 . . . Complete set lists for $1,600.

1965: Set features rookie cards of Dave Johnson (473), Steve Carlton (477) and Jim Hunter (526) . . . Lew Krausse (462) is photo of Pete Lovrich . . . Gene Freese (492) is again shown posing as a left-handed batter . . . Cards of Carlton and Pete Rose (207) list for $135 . . . Card of Mickey Mantle (350) lists for $300 . . . Complete set lists for $800.

1966: Set features rookie card of Jim Palmer (126) . . . For the third time (see 1962 and 1965) Gene Freese (319) is shown posing as a left-handed batter . . . Dick Ellsworth (447) is photo of Ken Hubbs (died February 13, 1964) . . . Card of Gaylord Perry (598) lists for $175 . . . Card of Willie McCovey (550) lists for $80 . . . Complete set lists for $2,500.

1967: Set features rookie cards of Rod Carew (569) and Tom Seaver (581) . . . Jim Fregosi (385) is shown posing as a left-handed batter . . . George Korince (72) is photo of James Brown but was later corrected on a second Korince card (526) . . . Card of Carew lists for $150 . . . Card of Maury Wills (570) lists for $65 . . . Complete set lists for $2,500.

1968: Set features rookie cards of Nolan Ryan (177) and Johnny Bench (247) . . . The special feature of The Sporting News All-Stars (361-380) includes eight players in the Hall of Fame . . . Card of Ryan lists for $135 . . . Card of Bench lists for $125 . . . Complete set lists for $1,200.

1969: Set features rookie card of Reggie Jackson (260) . . . There are two poses each for Clay Dalrymple (151) and Donn Clendenon (208) . . . Aurelio Rodriguez (653) is photo of Lenny Garcia (Angels' bat boy) . . . Card of Mickey Mantle (500) lists for $150 . . . Card of Jackson lists for $175 . . . Complete set lists for $1,200.

1970: Set features rookie cards of Vida Blue (21), Thurman Munson (189) and Bill Buckner (286) . . . Also included are two deceased players Miguel Fuentes (88) and Paul Edmondson (414) who died after cards went to press . . . Card of Johnny Bench (660) lists for $75 . . . Card of Pete Rose (580) lists for $75 . . . Complete set lists for $1,000.

1971: Set features rookie card of Steve Garvey (341) . . . the final series (644-752) is found in lesser quantity and includes rookie card (664) of three pitchers named Reynolds (Archie, Bob and Ken) . . . Card of Garvey lists for $65 . . . Card of Pete Rose (100) lists for $45 . . . Complete set lists for $1,000.

1972: There were 16 cards featuring photos of players in their boyhood years . . . Dave Roberts (91) is photo of Danny Coombs . . . Brewers Rookie Card (162) includes photos of Darrell Porter and Jerry Bell, which were reversed . . . Cards of Steve Garvey (686) and Rod Carew (695) list for $60 . . . Card of Pete Rose (559) lists for $50 . . . Complete set lists for $1,000.

1973: A special Home Run Card (1) depicted Babe Ruth, Hank Aaron and Willie Mays . . . Set features rookie card of Mike Schmidt (615) listing for $175 . . . Joe Rudi (360) is photo of Gene Tenace . . . Card of Pete Rose (130) lists for $18 . . . Card of Reggie Jackson (255) lists for $12.50 . . . Complete set lists for $600.

1974: Set features 15 San Diego Padres cards printed as "Washington, N.L." due to report of franchise move, later corrected . . . Also included was a 44-card Traded Series which updated team changes . . . Set features rookie card of Dave Winfield (456) . . . Card of Mike Schmidt (283) lists for $35 . . . Card of Winfield lists for $25 . . . Complete set lists for $325.

1975: Herb Washington (407) is the only card ever published with position "designated runner," featuring only base-running statistics . . . Set features rookie cards of Robin Yount (223), George Brett (228), Jim Rice (616), Gary Carter (620) and Keith Hernandez (623) . . . Don Wilson (455) died after cards went to press (January 5, 1975) . . . Card of Brett lists for $50 . . . Cards of Rice and Carter list for $35 . . . Complete set lists for $475 . . . TOPPS also tested the complete 660-card series in a smaller size (2¼" x 3 1/8") in certain areas of USA in a limited supply . . . Complete set of "Mini-Cards" lists for $700.

1976: As in 1974 there was a 44-card Traded Series . . . Set features five Father & Son cards (66-70) and ten All-Time All-Stars (341-350) . . . Card of Pete Rose (240) lists for $15 . . . Cards of Jim Rice (340), Gary Carter (441) and George Brett (19) list for $12 . . . Complete set lists for $225.

1977: Set features rookie cards of Andre Dawson (473) and Dale Murphy (476) . . . Reuschel Brother Combination (634) shows the two (Paul and Rick) misidentified . . . Dave Collins (431) is photo of Bob Jones . . . Card of Murphy lists for $65 . . . Card of Pete Rose (450) lists for $8.50 . . . Complete set lists for $250.

1978: Record Breakers (1-7) feature Lou Brock, Sparky Lyle, Willie McCovey, Brooks Robinson, Pete Rose, Nolan Ryan and Reggie Jackson . . . Set features rookie cards of Jack Morris (703), Lou Whitaker (704), Paul Molitor/Alan Trammell (707), Lance Parrish (708) and Eddie Murray (36) . . . Card of Murray lists for $35 . . . Card of Parrish lists for $35 . . . Complete set lists for $200.

1979: Bump Wills (369) was originally shown with Blue Jays affiliation but later corrected to Rangers . . . Set features rookie cards of Ozzie Smith (116), Pedro Guerrero (719), Lonnie Smith (722) and Terry Kennedy (724) . . . Larry Cox (489) is photo of Dave Rader . . . Card of Dale Murphy (39) lists for $8 . . . Cards of Ozzie Smith and Eddie Murray (640) list for $7.50 . . . Complete set lists for $135.

1980: Highlights (1-6) feature Hall-of-Famers Lou Brock, Carl Yastrzemski, Willie McCovey and Pete Rose . . . Set features rookie cards of Dave Stieb (77), Rickey Henderson (482) and Dan Quisenberry (667) . . . Card of Henderson lists for $28 . . . Card of Dale Murphy (274) lists for $5.50 . . . Complete set lists for $135.

1981: Set features rookie cards of Fernando Valenzuela (302), Kirk Gibson (315), Harold Baines (347) and Tim Raines (479) . . . Jeff Cox (133) is photo of Steve McCatty . . . John Littlefield (489) is photo of Mark Riggins . . . Card of Valenzuela lists for $7.50 . . . Card of Raines lists for $9 . . . Complete set lists for $80.

1982: Pascual Perez (383) printed with no position on front lists for $35, later corrected . . . Set features rookie cards of Cal Ripken (21), Jesse Barfield (203), Steve Sax (681) and Kent Hrbek (766) . . . Dave Rucker (261) is photo of Roger Weaver . . . Steve Bedrosian (502) is photo of Larry Owen . . . Card of Ripken lists for $12.50 . . . Cards of Barfield and Sax list for $5 . . . Complete set lists for $75.

1983: Record Breakers (1-6) feature Tony Armas, Rickey Henderson, Greg Minton, Lance Parrish, Manny Trillo and John Wathan . . . A series of Super Veterans features early and current photos of 34 leading players . . . Set features rookie cards of Tony Gwynn (482) and Wade Boggs (498) . . . Card of Boggs lists for $32 . . . Card of Gwynn lists for $16 . . . Complete set lists for $85.

1984: Highlights (1-6) salute eleven different players . . . A parade of superstars is included in Active Leaders (701-718) . . . Set features rookie card of Don Mattingly (8) listing for $35 . . . Card of Darryl Strawberry (182) lists for $10 . . . Complete set lists for $85.

1985: A Father & Son Feature (131-143) is again included . . . Set features rookie cards of Scott Bankhead (393), Mike Dunne (395), Shane Mack (398), John Marzano (399), Oddibe McDowell (400), Mark McGwire (401), Pat Pacillo (402), Cory Snyder (403) and Billy Swift (404) as part of salute to 1984 USA Baseball Team (389-404) that participated in Olympic Games plus rookie cards of Roger Clemens (181) and Eric Davis (627) . . . Card of McGwire lists for $20 . . . Card of Davis lists for $18 . . . Card of Clemens lists for $11 . . . Complete set lists for $95.

1986: Set includes Pete Rose Feature (2-7), which reproduces each of Rose's TOPPS cards from 1963 thru 1985 (four per card) . . . Bob Rodgers (141) should have been numbered 171 . . . Ryne Sandberg (690) is the only card with TOPPS logo omitted . . . Complete set lists for $24.

1987: Record Breakers (1-7) feature Roger Clemens, Jim Deshaies, Dwight Evans, Davey Lopes, Dave Righetti, Ruben Sierra and Todd Worrell . . . Jim Gantner (108) is shown with Brewers logo reversed . . . Complete set lists for $22.

1988: Record Breakers (1-7) include Vince Coleman, Don Mattingly, Mark McGwire, Eddie Murray, Phil & Joe Niekro, Nolan Ryan and Benny Santiago. Al Leiter (18) was originally shown with photo of minor leaguer Steve George and later corrected. Complete set lists for $20.00.

Pitching Record & Index

PLAYER	G	IP	W	L	R	ER	SO	BB	GS	CG	SHO	SV	ERA
ABERNATHY, TED	681	1148	63	69			765	592	34	7	5	148	3.46
ALLEN, NEIL	367	793.2	53	58	356	322	508	344	46	7	5	75	3.65
ANDERSON, CRAIG	82	192	7	23			94	81	17	2	0	5	5.11
ANDERSON, JOHN	24	45	0	0			19	14	1	0	0	1	6.40
ANDUJAR, JOAQUIN	369	2014	122	108			965	684	282	67	19	9	3.49
ARROYO, LUIS	244	533	40	32			336	208	36	10	1	44	3.92
AUST, DENNIS	15	17	0	1			4	8	0	0	0	2	5.82
BAIR, DOUG	443	693.2	47	37			526	313	2	0	0	76	3.54
BAKENHASTER, DAVE	2	3	0	0			1	2	0	0	0	0	6.00
BAKER, STEVE	84	236.2	7	16			131	127	26	0	0	5	5.13
BARE, RAY	88	340	16	26			145	120	49	9	3	1	4.79
BARGAR, GREG	11	28	2	1			11	15	4	0	0	0	7.07
BARLOW, MIKE	133	247	10	6			96	104	3	0	0	6	4.63
BARNES, FRANK	6	17	0	2			2	16	3	0	0	0	7.94
BAUTA, ED	97	149	6	6			89	70	0	0	0	11	4.35
BERTAINA, FRANK	99	412	19	29			280	214	76	6	5	0	3.84
BIBBY, JIM	340	1722.1	111	101			1079	723	239	56	19	8	3.76
BLAYLOCK, BOB	17	50	1	7			42	27	13	3	0	1	5.94
BLAYLOCK, GARY	41	126	6	4			81	58	13	3	0	2	4.79
BOKELMANN, DICK	34	68	3	4			27	38	1	0	0	0	4.90
BORBON, PEDRO	593	1026	69	39			409	251	4	0	0	80	3.52
BOYER, CLOYD	112	394	20	23			198	218	48	13	4	2	4.75
BRAZLE, AL	441	1375	97	64			554	492	117	41	5	60	3.31
BRECHEEN, HARRY	318	1905	133	92			901	536	240	125	25	18	2.92
BRILES, NELSON	452	2112	129	112			1163	547	279	64	17	22	3.43
BROGLIO, ERNIE	259	1337	77	74			849	587	184	52	18	2	3.74
BROSNAN, JIM	385	832	55	47			507	312	47	7	2	67	3.54
BRUNET, GEORGE	324	1431	69	93			921	581	213	39	15	4	3.62
BRUNO, TOM	69	123	7	7			80	61	4	0	0	1	4.24
BRYANT, RON	205	918	57	56			509	379	132	23	6	0	4.02
BURDETTE, LEW	626	3068	203	144			1074	528	373	158	33	31	3.66
BURRIS, RAY	447	2083.2	102	127			1023	720	290	47	10	4	4.10
BYERLY, BUD	237	492	22	22			209	167	17	4	0	14	3.70
CAMPBELL, BILL	693	1219.2	83	68	538	475	860	491	9	2	1	126	3.51
CAMPISI, SAL	50	63	2	2			35	47	0	0	0	4	2.71
CAPILLA, DOUG	136	293	12	18			178	173	31	1	0	2	4.33
CARLTON, STEVE	705	5054.2	323	229	2000	1749	4040	1742	687	251	55	2	3.11
CARROLL, CLAY	731	1353	96	73			681	442	28	1	0	143	2.94
CHAMBERS, CLIFF	189	897	48	53			374	361	113	37	6	1	4.29
CHENEY, TOM	115	466	19	29			345	245	71	13	8	2	3.77
CHITTUM, NELSON	40	67	3	1			30	24	2	0	0	0	3.90
CHLUPSA, BOB	15	18	0	2			11	27	0	0	0	0	9.00
CICOTTE, AL	102	260	10	13			149	119	16	0	0	4	4.36
CLARK, MIKE	35	61	0	2			27	35	4	0	0	1	5.31
CLARK, PHIL	14	15	0	1			6	11	4	0	0	0	7.80
CLEMONS, LANCE	19	35	2	1			23	21	4	0	0	0	6.18
CLEVELAND, REGGIE	428	1809	105	106			930	543	203	57	12	25	4.01
CLONINGER, TONY	352	1763	113	97	869	781	1120	798	247	63	13	6	4.07
COLLUM, JACKIE	171	464	32	28			171	173	37	11	2	12	4.15
CONROY, TIM	125	426.1	15	30	253	219	285	259	62	5	1	0	4.62
COSMAN, JIM	12	41	2	1			16	27	6	1	1	0	3.07
COX, DANNY	108	700.1	42	39	295	248	345	201	106	19	5	0	3.19
CRAIG, ROGER	368	1537	74	98			803	522	186	58	7	19	3.82
CRIMIAN, JACK	74	160	5	9			69	65	0	0	0	4	6.35
CUELLAR, MIKE	453	2807	185	130			1632	822	379	172	36	11	3.14
CULVER, GEORGE	335	789	48	49			451	352	57	7	2	23	3.62

PLAYER	G	IP	W	L	R	ER	SO	BB	GS	CG	SHO	SV	ERA
CUMBERLAND, JOHN	110	335	15	16			137	103	36	6	2	2	3.81
CURTIS, JOHN	438	1641	89	97			825	669	199	42	14	11	3.96
D'ACQUISTO, JOHN	266	780	24	51			600	544	92	7	1	15	4.56
DAVIS, JIM	154	407	22	26			197	179	39	4	1	10	4.00
DAWLEY, BILL	203	356.1	14	20	123	114	221	122	0	0	0	23	2.88
DAYLEY, KEN	139	303.2	14	26	169	141	309	104	33	0	0	16	4.18
DEAL, COT	45	90	3	4			34	48	8	0	0	0	6.50
DELEON, LUIS	195	309.1	17	17			233	68	0	0	0	31	3.03
DENNIS, DON	79	115	6	5			54	33	0	0	0	8	3.68
DENNY, JOHN	325	2149.2	123	108			1146	778	322	62	18	0	3.58
DICKSON, MURRY	625	3053	172	181			1281	1058	338	149	27	23	3.66
DIERKER, LARRY	356	2335	139	123			1493	711	329	106	25	1	3.30
DOWLING, DAVE	2	10	2	1			3	0	1	1	0	0	1.80
DRABOWSKY, MOE	589	1640	88	105			1162	702	154	30	6	55	3.71
DRESSLER, ROB	82	390	11	23			129	98	48	0	0	0	4.18
DULIBA, BOB	176	258	17	12			129	96	0	0	0	14	3.45
DURHAM, DON	25	88	2	11			58	45	12	1	0	1	5.83
EASTWICK, RAWLY	326	526	28	27			295	156	1	0	0	68	4.86
ERAUTT, ED	164	379.2	15	23			157	179	22	4	0	2	4.07
FALCONE, PETE	325	1434.1	70	90			865	671	217	25	7	1	5.14
FANOK, HARRY	16	35	2	1			35	24	0	0	0	1	3.99
FERRARESE, DON	183	507	19	36			350	295	50	12	2	5	3.40
FISHER, EDDIE	690	1541	85	70			812	438	63	7	2	81	3.41
FOLKERS, RICH	195	422	19	23			242	170	27	5	0	7	4.12
FORSCH, BOB	392	2371.1	143	116	1088	954	950	697	359	64	17	3	3.62
FOSTER, ALAN	217	1028	48	63			501	383	148	26	5	0	3.74
FRANCIS, EARL	103	405	16	23			263	181	52	5	1	1	3.78
FRAZIER, GEORGE	361	594.1	30	38	300	270	391	262	17	0	0	27	4.09
FRISELLA, DANNY	351	601	34	40			471	286	33	0	0	57	3.37
FULGHAM, JOHN	35	231	14	10			123	58	33	14	3	0	2.84
GARMAN, MIKE	303	434	22	27			213	202	8	0	0	42	3.63
GIBSON, BOB	528	3885	251	174			3117	1336	482	255	56	6	2.91
GILSON, HAL	15	25	0	2			20	12	0	0	0	2	5.04
GIUSTI, DAVE	668	1718	100	93			1103	570	133	35	9	145	3.60
GRANGER, WAYNE	451	640	35	35			303	201	0	0	0	108	3.14
GRANT, JIM	571	2441	145	119			1267	849	293	89	18	53	3.63
GREIF, BILL	231	715	31	67			442	287	97	18	4	19	4.42
GRIM, BOB	268	759	61	41			443	330	60	18	3	37	3.61
GRISSOM, MARV	356	810	47	45			459	343	52	12	0	58	3.41
GRZENDA, JOE	219	309	14	13			173	120	5	1	0	14	4.01
GUZMAN, SANTIAGO	12	32	1	2			29	18	5	1	0	0	4.50
HADDIX, HARVEY	453	2235	136	113			1575	601	285	99	20	21	3.63
HAGEN, KEVIN	13	29.2	3	2			18	12	5	0	0	0	4.25
HAMILTON, DAVE	301	703	39	41			434	317	57	4	1	31	3.85
HARTENSTEIN, CHUCK	187	297	17	19			135	89	0	0	0	23	3.85
HASSLER, ANDY	377	1113	44	70			625	516	112	26	5	29	3.85
HEARN, JIM	396	1704	109	89			669	655	229	63	10	8	3.81
HIGGINS, DENNIS	241	205	22	23			179	134	6	2	0	46	4.07
HILGENDORF, TOM	184	314	19	14			173	127	0	2	0	12	3.04
HOBBIE, GLEN	284	1263	62	81			682	495	170	45	11	6	4.20
HOERNER, JOE	493	563	39	34			412	120	0	0	0	99	2.99
HOOD, DON	297	847.1	34	35			374	364	72	6	2	6	3.79
HORTON, RICKY	128	315.2	16	9			184	99	30	2	0	5	3.82
HRABOSKY, AL	545	721.1	64	35			548	315	1	0	0	97	3.11
HUGHES, DICK	68	307	20	9	108	102	230	76	34	13	4	8	2.79
HUMPHREYS, BOB	319	568	27	21			364	219	4	0	0	20	3.34

Left table

PLAYER	G	IP	W	L	R	ER	SO	BB	GS	CG	SHO	SV	ERA
HUTCHINSON, FREDDY	242	1465	95	71			591	388	169	81	13	7	3.72
JACKSON, AL	302	1389	67	99			738	407	184	54	14	10	3.98
JACKSON, LARRY	558	3262	194	183			1709	824	429	149	37	20	3.40
JACOBS, TONY	2	4	0	0			3	1	0	0	0	0	11.25
JASTER, LARRY	138	597	35	33			313	178	80	15	7	3	3.65
JEFFCOAT, HAL	245	697	39	37			239	257	51	13	1	25	4.22
JOHNSON, JERRY	365	771	48	51			489	389	39	7	2	41	4.31
JONES, GORDON	171	379	15	18			232	120	21	4	2	12	4.16
JONES, SAM	322	1644	102	101			1376	822	222	76	17	9	3.59
KAAT, JIM	898	4527.2	283	237			2461	1083	625	180	31	18	3.45
KELLNER, ALEX	321	1851	101	112			816	747	250	99	7	5	4.41
KENNEDY, MONTE	249	960	42	55			411	495	127	48	2	4	3.84
KEPSHIRE, KURT	49	262.1	16	14			138	115	45	2	0	0	4.15
KINDER, ELLIS	484	1480	102	71			749	539	122	56	10	102	3.43
KLINE, RON	736	2078	114	144			989	731	203	44	8	108	3.86
KNOWLES, DAROLD	765	1091	66	74			681	480	8	1	1	143	3.12
KONSTANTY, JIM	433	947	66	48			268	269	36	14	2	74	3.46
KRAUSSE, LEW	321	1285	68	91			721	493	167	21	5	21	4.00
KUZAVA, BOB	213	862	49	44			446	415	99	34	6	13	4.05
LAGROW, LERRIN	309	778	34	55			375	312	67	19	0	54	4.12
LAHTI, JEFF	205	286	17	11	109	99	137	111	1	0	0	20	3.12
LAMABE, JACK	285	710	33	41	370	341	434	238	49	7	3	15	4.25
LANIER, MAX	327	1619	108	82			821	611	204	91	21	17	3.01
LAPALME, PAUL	253	616	24	45			277	272	51	10	2	14	4.42
LAPOINT, DAVE	191	898.2	46	49	453	396	532	358	131	5	1	2	3.97
LAWRENCE, BROOKS	275	1041	69	62			481	385	127	42	9	22	4.25
LERSCH, BARRY	169	570	18	32			317	172	53	9	1	6	3.82
LIDDLE, DON	117	428	28	18			198	203	54	13	3	4	3.74
LINZY, FRANK	516	817	62	55			358	282	2	1	0	111	2.85
LITTELL, MARK	316	531.2	32	31			466	304	19	2	0	56	3.32
LITTLE, JEFF	40	55.1	3	3			43	36	2	0	0	2	4.07
LITTLEFIELD, DICK	243	761	33	54			495	413	83	16	0	9	4.72
LITTLEFIELD, JOHN	94	130	7	8			43	48	0	0	0	11	3.39
LOCKE, BOBBY	165	416	16	15			194	165	23	2	0	10	4.02
LOPEZ, AURELIO	433	872.1	60	35			614	355	14	0	0	92	3.52
MABE, BOB	51	143	7	11			82	61	14	4	0	3	4.78
MACKENZIE, KEN	129	207	8	10			142	63	1	0	0	3	4.83
MADISON, DAVE	74	158	8	7			70	103	6	0	0	5	5.70
MAGLIE, SAL	303	1721	119	62			862	652	232	93	25	14	3.15
MAHAFFEY, ART	185	998	59	64			639	368	148	46	9	1	4.18
MARTIN, JOHN	91	290.2	17	14			120	95	32	5	1	1	3.93
MARTIN, MORRIE	250	604	38	34			245	251	42	8	1	15	4.29
MARTINEZ, SILVIO	107	583	31	32			230	237	87	14	4	0	3.87
MATHEWS, GREG	23	145.1	11	8	61	59	67	44	22	1	0	0	3.65
MCCOOL, BILL	292	528	32	42			471	272	20	2	0	58	3.60
MCDANIEL, LINDY	987	2140	141	119			1361	623	74	18	4	172	3.45
MCDERMOTT, MICKEY	291	1316	69	69			757	838	156	54	11	14	3.91
MCENANEY, WILL	269	350	12	17			148	95	0	0	0	29	3.75
MCGLOTHEN, LYNN	318	1498	86	93			939	572	201	41	13	2	3.98
MERRITT, LLOYD	44	65	1	2			35	28	1	0	0	7	3.32
METZGER, BUTCH	191	293	18	9			175	140	1	0	0	23	3.75
MIKKELSEN, PETE	364	653	45	40	276	241	436	250	3	0	0	49	3.38
MILLER, BOB L.	694	1552	69	81			895	608	99	7	0	52	3.37
MILLER, STU	704	1694	105	103			1164	600	93	24	5	154	3.24
MIZELL, WILMER	268	1528	90	88			918	680	230	61	15	0	3.85
MOFORD, HERB	50	158	5	13			78	64	14	6	0	3	5.01
MOORE, DONNIE	375	596.1	36	36			377	165	41	0	0	80	3.64
MUFFETT, BILLY	125	377	16	23			188	132	32	7	1	15	4.32
MUNGER, GEORGE	273	1229	77	56			564	500	161	54	13	12	3.83
MURA, STEVE	167	632.2	30	39			360	289	83	12	2	5	3.99

Right table

PLAYER	G	IP	W	L	R	ER	SO	BB	GS	CG	SHO	SV	ERA
NAGY, MIKE	87	420	20	13			170	210	62	11	1	1	4.14
NELSON, MEL	93	174	4	10			98	69	11	1	0	5	4.40
NORMAN, FRED	403	1938	104	103			1303	815	268	56	15	8	3.64
NUNN, HOWIE	46	69	3	3			50	42	0	0	0	4	5.09
NYE, RICH	113	478	26	31			267	140	63	16	1	4	3.71
O'BRIEN, DAN	13	29	1	3			17	11	2	0	0	3	5.90
O'NEAL, RANDY	69	235.2	10	9	118	100	132	86	26	2	0	3	3.82
OLMSTED, AL	5	35	1	1			14	14	5	0	0	0	2.83
OSTEEN, CLAUDE	541	3460	196	195			1612	940	488	140	40	1	3.30
OTTEN, JIM	64	118	1	6			75	67	5	0	0	0	5.49
OWNBEY, RICK	22	104	2	8			58	72	16	2	0	0	4.24
PAINE, PHIL	95	149	10	1			101	80	0	0	0	1	3.38
PALMER, LOWELL	106	317	5	18			239	202	25	2	1	0	5.28
PARKER, HARRY	134	315	15	21			172	128	30	1	0	12	3.86
PATTERSON, DARYL	142	231	11	9			142	119	3	0	0	11	4.09
PENA, ORLANDO	427	1203	56	77			818	352	93	21	4	40	3.70
PERRY, PAT	52	81	3	3	31	29	35	37	0	0	0	2	3.22
PICHE, RON	134	221	10	16			157	123	11	3	0	12	4.19
POHOLSKY, TOM	159	754	31	52			316	192	104	30	5	0	3.93
POLLET, HOWIE	403	2106	131	116			934	745	277	116	25	20	3.51
PRESKO, JOE	128	492	25	37			202	188	61	15	2	5	4.59
PROLY, MIKE	267	546	22	29			185	195	18	2	0	22	3.23
PURKEY, BOB	386	2115	129	115			793	510	276	92	13	3	3.79
RAFFENSBERGER, KEN	396	2152	119	154			806	449	282	133	31	16	3.60
RASMUSSEN, H. 'ERIC'	238	1016.2	50	77			489	309	144	22	12	5	3.85
REED, RON	751	2475.1	146	140			1481	633	236	55	8	103	3.46
REUSS, JERRY	537	3218.2	194	163	1438	1251	1744	1018	468	123	37	11	3.50
REYNOLDS, BOB	140	254	14	16			167	82	10	0	0	21	3.59
REYNOLDS, KEN	103	374	14	29			197	196	51	4	1	1	3.68
RIBANT, DENNIS	149	519	24	29			241	126	56	12	0	9	3.87
RICHARDSON, GORDON	69	118	6	6			86	37	7	1	0	4	4.04
RICHERT, PETE	429	1166	80	73			925	424	122	22	3	51	3.19
RICKETTS, DICK	12	56	1	6			25	30	9	0	0	0	5.79
RINCON, ANDY	20	107	8	5			46	37	15	3	1	0	3.11
ROE, PREACHER	333	1916	127	84			956	504	261	101	17	10	3.43
ROMONOSKY, JOHN	32	101	3	4			63	51	9	0	0	10	5.17
ROOT, CHARLIE	632	3197	201	160			1459	889	341	177	21	40	3.59
RUCKER, DAVE	156	266.1	16	16			140	124	10	1	0	16	3.68
RYBA, MIKE	240	784	52	34			307	247	36	16	2	7	3.66
SADECKI, RAY	563	2500.1	135	131			1614	922	327	85	20	7	3.78
SANTORINI, AL	127	494	17	38			268	194	70	5	4	3	4.28
SCHEIB, CARL	267	1072	45	65	657	579	290	493	107	47	6	17	4.88
SCHMIDT, WILLARD	194	588	31	29			323	278	55	11	1	2	3.92
SCHULTZ, BARNEY	227	347	20	20			264	116	3	0	0	35	3.63
SEGUI, DIEGO	639	1808	92	101			1298	786	171	28	7	71	3.67
SHANTZ, BOBBY	537	1936	119	99			1072	643	171	78	15	48	3.38
SHAW, DON	138	188	13	14			123	101	1	0	0	6	4.02
SHIRLEY, BOB	399	1432	66	94			777	521	161	16	2	18	3.75
SIEBERT, SONNY	401	2152	140	114			1511	692	307	67	21	2	3.21
SIMMONS, CURT	569	3349	193	183			1697	1063	461	163	36	5	3.54
SMITH, BILLY G.	32	68	1	6			34	17	8	2	0	1	4.24
SMITH, BOB G.	91	167	5	9			93	83	7	0	0	6	4.04
SMITH, FRANK	271	496	35	33			277	181	2	0	0	44	3.81
SOFF, RAY	30	38.1	4	2	17	14	22	13	0	0	0	4	3.29
SOLOMON, EDDIE	191	718	36	42			337	247	95	2	2	4	4.00
SORENSEN, LARY	311	1671.2	90	99			539	387	230	69	10	3	4.12
SOSA, ELIAS	601	919.1	59	51			538	334	3	0	0	83	3.32
SPINKS, SCIPIO	35	202	7	12			154	107	29	3	0	7	3.75
SPRAGUE, ED	198	409	17	23			188	206	23	3	0	9	3.83

Name													
STALEY, GERRY	640	1981	134	111		304	727	529	186	58	9	61	3.70
STALLARD, TRACY	183	765	30	57			477	343	104	21	3	4	4.16
STOBBS, CHUCK	459	1920	107	130			897	735	238	65	7	19	4.29
STONE, DEAN	215	687	29	39			380	373	85	19	5	12	4.47
STUPER, JOHN	111	495	32	28			191	183	76	9	1	1	3.96
SURKONT, MAX	236	1194	61	76			571	481	149	53	7	8	4.38
SUTTER, BRUCE	623	955.1	67	67	344		821	298	0	0	0	286	2.75
SUTTON, JOHNNY	31	68	2	1			27	24	0	0	0	0	3.57
SYKES, BOB	116	457	23	26			215	190	61	10	3	2	4.65
TAYLOR, CHUCK	305	607	28	20			282	162	21	6	2	31	3.07
TAYLOR, RON	491	799	45	43			464	209	17	3	0	72	3.93
TERLECKY, GREG	20	30	0	1			13	12	0	0	0	0	4.50
TERRY, RALPH	338	1850	107	99			1000	446	257	75	20	11	3.62
THOMAS, ROY	174	398	19	11			275	185	13	0	0	7	3.75
THOMPSON, MIKE	54	165	1	15			113	128	29	0	0	0	4.85
TIEFENAUER, BOB	179	316	9	25			204	87	0	0	15	23	3.84
TORREZ, MIKE	494	3042	185	160			1404	1371	458	117	15	0	3.96
TOTH, PAUL	43	193	9	12			82	54	21	5	2	0	3.78
TUDOR, JOHN	204	1342.2	85	58	544	487	775	366	192	44	14	1	3.26
TUNNELL, LEE	90	396.2	17	24			224	160	57	5	3	1	4.06
UNDERWOOD, TOM	379	1586.1	86	87			948	662	203	35	6	18	3.89
URBAN, JACK	69	272	15	15			113	103	37	8	1	1	4.83
URREA, JOHN	139	364	17	18			202	160	27	3	1	9	3.73
VON OHLEN, DAVE	123	161.2	7	7	67	57	56	60	0	0	3	4	3.17
VUCKOVICH, PETE	280	1422	91	65			870	534	180	38	8	10	3.68
WADE, BEN	118	371	19	17			235	181	25	5	1	10	4.34
WALKER, TOM	191	415	18	23			262	142	17	2	0	11	3.86
WALLACE, MIKE	123	194	11	3			112	118	4	1	0	3	3.94
WASHBURN, RAY	239	1208	72	64			700	354	166	25	10	5	3.54
WASLEWSKI, GARY	152	411	11	26			229	197	42	5	1	9	3.44
WEHMEIER, HERMAN	361	1804	92	108			794	852	240	79	9	9	4.79
WERLE, BILL	185	666	29	39			283	194	60	18	9	15	4.69
WIGHT, BILL	347	1562	77	99			574	714	198	66	15	8	3.95
WILHELM, HOYT	1070	2253	143	122			1610	778	52	20	5	227	2.52
WILKS, TED	385	913	59	30			403	283	44	22	5	46	3.26
WILLIAMS, STAN	482	1763	109	94			1305	748	208	42	11	43	3.48
WILLIS, RON	188	239	11	12			128	119	0	0	0	19	3.31
WISE, RICK	506	3125	188	181			1647	804	455	138	30	61	3.69
WOODESHICK, HAL	427	847	44	62			484	389	62	7	1	61	3.56
WORRELL, TODD	91	125.1	12	10	36	31	90	48	0	0	0	41	2.23
WRIGHT, MEL	58	83	2	4			36	27	0	0	0	3	7.70
YOUNG, CY	906	7357	511	313			2803	1217	816	750	77	18	2.63
YUHAS, EDDIE	56	100	12	2			39	35	2	0	1	6	2.88
ZACHARY, CHRIS	108	321	10	29			184	122	40	1	1	2	4.51

Batting Record & Index

PLAYER	G	AB	R	H	2B	3B	HR	RBI	SB	SLG	BB	SO	AVG
AGEE, TOMMIE	1129	3912	558	999	170	27	130	433	167	.412	342	918	.255
ALLEN, RICHIE	1749	6332	1099	1848	320	79	351	1119	133	.534	894	1556	.292
ALSTON, WALTER	1667	5789	780	1777	236	50	31	427	156	.381	311	377	.307
ALTMAN, GEORGE	991	3091	409	832	132	34	101	403	52	.432	268	572	.269
ALVARADO, LUIS	463	1160	116	248	43	4	5	84	11	.271	47	160	.214
ALYEA, BRANT	371	866	100	214	33	2	38	148	5	.421	100	210	.247
AMARO, RUBEN	940	2155	211	505	75	13	8	156	11	.292	227	280	.234
ANDERSON, DWAIN	149	306	33	62	6	2	1	14	2	.242	70	70	.201
ANDERSON, MIKE	721	1490	159	367	42	11	28	134	8	.362	61	343	.246
AYALA, BENNY	425	865	114	217	18	4	38	145	2	.434	54	136	.251
BEAUCHAMP, JIM	393	661	79	153	18	4	14	90	6	.334	54	150	.231
BENSON, VERN	55	104	17	21	5	1	1	12	0	.356	13	22	.202
BILKO, STEVE	600	1738	220	432	85	13	76	276	0	.444	234	395	.249
BILLINGS, DICK	400	1231	101	280	44	1	16	142	6	.304	87	207	.227
BLADES, RAY	767	2415	467	726	133	51	50	340	33	.460	331	310	.301
BLASINGAME, DON	1444	5296	731	1366	178	62	21	308	105	.327	552	462	.258
BLOOMFIELD, CLYDE	8	7		1						.143			.143
BOLLWEG, DON	195	452	62	110	22	7	7	53	2	.396	60	68	.243
BONDS, BOBBY	1849	7043	1258	1886	302	66	332	1024	461	.471	914	1757	.268
BOSETTI, RICK	445	1543	172	385	70	8	17	133	30	.327	79	188	.250
BOYER, KEN	2034	7455	1104	2143	318	68	282	1141	105	.462	713	1017	.287
BRADFORD, BUDDY	697	1603	224	363	50	8	52	175	36	.412	184	411	.226
BRANDT, JACKIE	1221	3895	540	1020	175	37	112	485	45	.367	351	574	.262
BRAUN, STEVE	1425	3650	466	989	155	19	52	388	45	.367	579	433	.271
BRESSOUD, ED	1186	3672	443	925	155	40	94	365	9	.401	184	723	.252
BRIDGES, ROCKY	919	2272	245	562	80	11	16	187	10	.313	205	229	.247
BRINKMAN, ED	1845	6045	552	1355	201	38	149	461	30	.299	444	845	.224
BROCK, LOU	2616	10332	1610	3023	486	141	149	900	938	.410	761	1730	.293
BROWNE, BYRON	349	869	94	205	37	10	32	102	5	.405	101	273	.236
BRUMMER, GLENN	178	347	23	87	16	0	1	27	4	.305	25	54	.251
BUCHA, JOHNNY	84	195	18	40	10	0	1	15	0	.272	25	21	.205
BUCHEK, JERRY	421	1177	96	259	35	11	22	108	5	.375	75	312	.220
BURBRINK, NELSON	58	170	11	47	8	1	0	15	1	.335	14	13	.276
BURDA, BOB	388	634	53	142	21	0	13	78	2	.319	70	65	.225
BURKE, LEO	165	301	33	72	17	2	5	45	1	.365	21	79	.239
BURTON, ELLIS	215	556	79	120	24	4	17	59	11	.365	65	117	.216
BUSSE, RAY	68	155	12	23	8	2	0	9	0	.265	11	54	.148
CAMPBELL, DAVE	428	1252	128	267	54	4	20	89	29	.311	102	254	.213
CANNIZZARO, CHRIS	740	1950	132	458	46	6	18	169	1	.309	221	354	.235
CARBO, BERNIE	1010	2733	372	722	140	9	96	358	51	.427	538	611	.264
CARDENAL, JOSE	2017	6964	936	1913	333	46	138	775	329	.395	608	807	.275
CARMEL, DUKE	124	227	22	48	7	3	4	23	2	.322	27	60	.211
CASTIGLIONE, PETE	545	1670	205	426	62	11	24	150	10	.349	103	126	.255
CATER, DANNY	1289	4451	491	1276	191	29	66	519	26	.375	254	406	.276
CEDENO, CESAR	1969	7232	1079	2069	434	59	199	970	549	.445	657	925	.286
CEPEDA, ORLANDO	2124	7927	1131	2351	417	27	379	1365	142	.483	588	1169	.297
CIMOLI, GINO	969	3054	370	808	133	48	44	321	21	.399	221	474	.265
CLARK, JACK	1235	4405	702	1213	235	35	194	705	62	.477	625	705	.275
CLEMENS, DOUG	452	920	99	211	34	7	12	88	6	.321	114	166	.229
CLENDENON, DONN	1362	4648	594	1273	192	57	159	682	90	.442	379	1140	.274
COLE, DICK	456	1215	106	303	50	10	4	107	2	.312	132	124	.249
COLEMAN, VINCE	305	1236	201	309	33	18	1	69	217	.308	110	213	.250
COLUCCIO, BOB	370	1095	141	241	38	15	26	114	33	.353	152	202	.220
COOPER, WALKER	1473	4702	573	1341	240	40	173	812	18	.464	309	357	.285

PLAYER	G	AB	R	H	2B	3B	HR	RBI	SB	SLG	BB	SO	AVG
CRAWFORD, WILLIE	1210	3435	507	921	152	35	86	419	47	.408	431	664	.268
CROSBY, ED	297	677	67	149	22	4	0	44	0	.264	55	74	.220
CROWE, GEORGE	702	1727	215	467	70	12	81	299	3	.466	159	246	.270
CRUZ, HECTOR	624	1607	186	385	71	9	39	200	5	.353	175	314	.225
CRUZ, JOSE	2189	7472	980	2147	372	90	153	1032	313	.423	854	958	.278
CUNNINGHAM, JOE	1141	3362	525	980	177	26	64	436	16	.417	599	368	.291
DARK, ALVIN	1828	7219	1064	2089	358	72	126	757	59	.411	430	534	.289
DAVALILLO, VIC	1458	4017	509	1122	160	37	36	329	123	.364	212	422	.279
DAVANON, JERRY	262	499	73	117	21	5	3	50	21	.315	68	80	.234
DAVIS, RON E.	295	853	96	199	44	6	10	79	9	.334	56	160	.233
DAVIS, WILLIE	2429	9174	1217	2561	395	138	182	1053	397	.412	408	977	.279
DAY, BOOTS	471	1151	146	289	28	6	8	98	15	.312	95	141	.256
DECINCES, DOUG	1512	5347	712	1397	287	29	221	815	55	.450	548	815	.261
DEJESUS, IVAN	1348	4571	593	1162	175	48	42	323	194	.327	464	657	.254
DEL GRECO, BOBBY	731	1982	271	451	95	11	42	169	16	.352	271	372	.229
DESA, JOE	35	55	7	11	2	0	0	7	0	.345	3	8	.200
DIERING, CHUCK	752	1648	217	411	76	14	14	141	16	.338	237	250	.249
DRIESSEN, DAN	1676	5379	734	1440	277	23	151	749	154	.412	745	705	.268
DUNCAN, TAYLOR	112	331	27	86	15	2	5	39	2	.344	21	39	.260
DURHAM, JOE	93	202	25	38	2	0	5	20	1	.272	20	50	.188
DURHAM, LEON	862	3006	436	844	160	38	116	458	104	.475	377	551	.281
DUROCHER, LEO	1637	5350	575	1320	210	56	24	567	31	.320	377	480	.247
DUSAK, ERV	413	1035	168	251	32	6	24	106	12	.355	142	188	.243
DWYER, JIM	1043	2128	304	543	95	16	56	268	22	.394	299	295	.255
DYBZINSKI, JERRY	463	905	108	213	32	5	6	93	32	.292	70	109	.235
EDWARDS, JOHNNY	1470	4577	430	1106	202	32	81	524	15	.353	465	635	.242
ELLIOTT, HARRY	92	176	15	45	10	1	2	18	1	.358	14	17	.256
ENNIS, DEL	1903	7524	985	2063	258	69	288	1284	45	.472	597	719	.284
ESSEGIAN, CHUCK	404	1018	139	260	45	4	47	150	2	.446	97	233	.255
FAIRLY, RON	2442	7184	931	1913	307	33	215	1044	35	.408	1052	877	.266
FENWICK, BOB	41	56	7	10	3	0	0	3	1	.232	3	15	.179
FERGUSON, JOE	1013	2951	407	719	121	11	122	445	22	.416	565	607	.244
FIORE, MIKE	254	556	75	126	18	1	13	50	5	.333	124	115	.227
FLOOD, CURT	1759	6357	851	1861	271	44	85	636	88	.389	444	609	.293
FORD, CURT	96	226	32	59	17	2	3	32	14	.381	27	30	.261
FRANCONA, TITO	1719	5121	650	1395	224	34	125	656	46	.403	544	694	.272
FRANKS, HERMAN	188	403	35	80	18	3	3	43	2	.275	57	37	.199
FRAZIER, JOE	217	282	31	68	15	2	10	45	0	.415	35	46	.241
FREED, ROGER	344	717	49	176	35	1	22	109	1	.381	95	166	.245
FREESE, GENE	1115	3446	429	877	161	28	115	432	21	.418	243	535	.254
FUSSELMAN, LES	43	71	6	12	4	0	0	3	0	.268	9	9	.169
GAGLIANO, PHIL	702	1411	150	336	50	7	14	159	5	.313	163	184	.238
GARAGIOLA, JOE	676	1872	198	481	82	16	42	255	3	.385	267	173	.257
GARRETT, WAYNE	1092	3285	438	786	107	22	61	340	38	.341	561	529	.239
GLAVIANO, TOMMY	389	1008	191	259	55	6	24	108	11	.297	208	173	.257
GONZALEZ, JULIO	370	969	90	228	32	8	4	66	13	.297	36	132	.235
GOTAY, JULIO	389	988	106	257	38	3	7	70	6	.323	61	127	.260
GRAMMAS, ALEX	913	2073	236	512	90	10	12	163	17	.317	193	247	.247
GRAY, DICK	124	305	43	73	7	1	12	41	4	.420	33	52	.239
GREEN, DAVID	475	1368	164	366	46	17	30	179	68	.392	82	273	.268
GREEN, GENE	408	1151	130	307	49	7	40	160	2	.441	89	185	.267
GRIEVE, TOM	670	1907	209	474	76	10	65	254	7	.401	135	424	.249
GRIMM, CHARLIE	2164	7917	908	2299	394	108	79	1078	57	.397	578	410	.290
GROAT, DICK	1929	7484	829	2138	352	67	39	707	14	.366	490	512	.286
GUERRERO, MARIO	697	2251	167	578	79	12	7	170	8	.312	84	152	.257

HAGUE, JOE	430	1195	141	286	41	10	40	163	4	.391	177	222	.239
HAHN, DON	454	997	104	235	38	4	7	74	11	.303	122	158	.236
HANEY, FRED	622	1977	338	544	66	21	8	228	50	.342	282	123	.275
HANEY, LARRY	480	919	68	198	30	1	12	73	3	.289	44	175	.215
HARMON, CHUCK	289	592	90	141	15	8	7	59	25	.326	46	57	.238
HARPER, BRIAN	175	337	30	82	13	1	11	44	1	.386	10	34	.243
HARRIS, VIC	579	1610	168	349	57	15	13	121	36	.295	160	281	.217
HATTON, GRADY	1312	4206	562	1068	166	33	91	533	42	.374	646	430	.254
HEATH, MIKE	853	2818	316	698	113	20	55	325	38	.361	189	375	.248
HEIDEMANN, JACK	426	1093	94	231	27	4	9	75	5	.268	78	203	.211
HEINTZELMAN, TOM	90	140	17	34	5	0	3	12	0	.343	14	22	.243
HEISE, BOBBY	499	1144	104	283	43	3	1	86	3	.293	47	77	.247
HEMUS, SOLLY	961	2694	459	736	137	41	51	263	21	.411	456	247	.273
HENDRICK, GEORGE	1914	6840	915	1910	332	27	259	1067	59	.449	546	975	.279
HERNANDEZ, KEITH	1721	6090	969	1840	372	58	128	900	96	.445	917	795	.302
HERNDON, LARRY	1372	4478	557	1222	168	74	94	483	91	.406	307	721	.273
HERR, TOM	873	3162	422	874	150	31	16	349	130	.359	359	322	.276
HERZOG, WHITEY	634	1614	213	414	60	20	25	172	13	.365	241	261	.257
HICKMAN, JIM	1421	3974	518	1002	163	25	159	560	17	.426	491	832	.252
HICKS, JIM	93	141	16	23	1	3	5	14	0	.319	18	48	.163
HILL, MARC	715	1790	144	401	62	3	34	198	1	.319	184	240	.224
HOPP, JOHNNY	1393	4260	698	1262	216	74	46	458	128	.414	465	378	.296
HORNSBY, ROGERS	2259	8173	1579	2930	541	169	301	1584	135	.577	1038	679	.358
HOUSEHOLDER, PAUL	426	1236	140	295	56	10	28	127	35	.368	115	232	.239
HOWE, ART	887	2623	268	682	139	23	43	293	10	.380	275	287	.260
HOWERTON, BILL	247	650	95	178	39	12	22	106	1	.472	92	125	.274
HUGHES, TERRY	54	86	6	18	3	0	1	7	0	.279	7	22	.209
HUNT, RANDY	14	19	1	3	0	0	0	1	0	.158	0	5	.158
HUNT, RON	1483	5235	745	1429	223	23	39	370	65	.347	555	382	.273
HUNTZ, STEVE	237	636	81	131	19	1	16	60	1	.314	108	122	.206
HURDLE, CLINT	512	1388	161	359	81	12	32	193	1	.403	176	260	.259
IORG, DANE	743	1647	149	455	103	11	14	216	5	.378	107	180	.276
JABLONSKI, RAY	812	2562	297	687	126	11	83	438	16	.423	196	330	.268
JAMES, CHARLEY	510	1406	158	358	56	9	29	172	7	.369	48	260	.255
JAVIER, JULIAN	1622	5722	722	1469	216	55	78	506	135	.355	314	812	.257
JOHNSON, ALEX	1322	4623	550	1331	180	33	78	525	103	.392	244	626	.288
JOHNSON, BILLY	964	3253	419	882	141	33	61	487	13	.391	347	290	.271
JOHNSON, BOB W.	874	2307	254	628	88	11	44	230	24	.377	156	291	.272
JOHNSON, DARRELL	134	320	24	75	6	1	2	28	1	.278	26	39	.234
JONES, NIPPY	412	1381	146	369	60	12	25	209	4	.382	71	102	.267
JORGENSEN, MIKE	1633	3421	429	833	132	13	95	426	58	.373	532	589	.243
JUTZE, SKIP	254	656	45	141	14	3	3	51	1	.259	34	86	.215
KASKO, EDDIE	1077	3546	411	935	146	13	22	261	31	.331	265	353	.264
KATT, RAY	417	1071	92	248	29	4	32	120	2	.356	74	164	.232
KAZAK, EDDIE	218	605	69	165	22	6	11	71	0	.383	52	45	.273
KEANE, JOHNNY	No major league statistics												
KEELY, BOB	2	1	0	0	0	0	0	0	0	.000	0	0	.000
KELLEHER, MICK	622	1081	108	230	32	6	0	65	9	.253	74	133	.213
KENNEDY, TERRY	962	3373	347	916	177	10	82	477	3	.403	238	565	.272
KERNEK, GEORGE	30	81	11	21	3	2	0	6	1	.346	6	13	.259
KESSINGER, DON	2078	7651	899	1931	254	80	14	527	100	.312	684	759	.252
KING, CHICK	45	76	11	18	0	1	0	5	0	.263	8	18	.237
KING, JIM	1125	2918	374	699	112	19	117	401	23	.411	363	401	.240
KISSELL, GEORGE	No major league statistics												
KLUTTZ, CLYDE	656	1903	172	510	90	8	19	212	5	.354	132	119	.268
KNICELY, ALAN	194	439	40	95	14	0	11	55	0	.323	51	107	.216
KOLB, GARY	293	450	63	94	9	6	6	29	10	.296	46	104	.209
KUBIAK, TED	977	2447	238	565	61	21	13	202	13	.289	271	272	.231
LAGA, MIKE	90	247	25	58	15	0	11	36	1	.429	16	74	.235
LAKE, STEVE	157	326	26	72	12	1	6	39	1	.319	8	41	.221
LANDRITH, HOBIE	772	1929	179	450	69	5	34	203	5	.327	253	188	.233
LANDRUM, DON	456	1160	151	272	36	8	12	75	36	.310	104	200	.234

LANDRUM, TITO	513	854	105	219	36	11	12	99	15	.367	71	160	.256
LAVALLIERE, MIKE	128	344	20	76	11	2	3	36	0	.291	45	42	221
LAWLESS, TOM	196	359	43	81	13	1	1	17	33	.276	24	58	.226
LEE, LERON	614	1617	173	404	83	13	31	152	19	.375	133	315	.250
LEWIS, JOHNNY	226	771	97	175	24	6	22	74	8	.359	95	194	.297
LEZCANO, SIXTO	1291	4134	560	1122	184	34	148	591	37	.440	576	768	.271
LILLIS, BOB	817	2328	198	549	68	9	3	137	23	.277	99	116	.236
LINTZ, LARRY	350	616	137	140	13	1	0	27	128	.252	97	101	.227
LOCKMAN, WHITEY	1666	5940	836	1658	222	49	114	563	43	.391	552	383	.279
LONG, JEOFF	56	83	5	16	1	0	1	9	0	.241	10	34	.193
LOWREY, HARRY	1401	4317	564	1177	186	45	37	479	48	.362	403	226	.273
MARIS, ROGER	1463	5101	826	1325	195	42	275	851	21	.476	652	733	.260
MARTINEZ, MARTY	436	945	97	230	19	11	0	57	7	.287	70	107	.243
MARTINEZ, TED	657	1480	165	355	50	16	7	108	29	.309	55	213	.240
MAUCH, GENE	304	737	93	176	25	7	5	62	6	.312	104	82	.239
MAXVILL, DAL	1423	3443	302	748	79	24	6	252	7	.259	370	538	.217
MCBRIDE, BAKE	1071	3853	548	1153	167	55	63	430	183	..394	248	457	.299
MCCARVER, TIM	1909	5529	590	1501	242	57	97	645	61	.388	548	422	.271
MCGEE, WILLIE	691	2703	379	806	101	52	32	311	181	.410	138	404	.298
MEJIAS, SAM	334	348	51	86	13	2	4	31	8	.330	16	51	.247
MELENDEZ, LUIS	641	1477	167	366	50	13	9	122	18	.318	109	175	.248
MIKSIS, EDDIE	1042	3053	383	722	95	17	44	228	52	.322	215	313	.236
MILLS, BUSTER	415	1379	200	396	62	19	14	163	24	.390	131	137	.287
MINOSO, MINNIE	1835	6597	1136	1963	336	83	186	1023	205	.459	814	584	.298
MIZE, JOHNNEY	1884	6443	1118	2011	367	83	359	1337	28	562	856	524	.312
MOON, WALLY	1457	4843	737	1399	212	60	142	661	89	.445	644	591	.289
MORALES, JERRY	1441	4528	516	1173	199	36	95	570	37	.382	366	567	.259
MORGAN, BOBBY	671	2088	286	487	96	11	53	217	18	.366	327	381	.233
MORGAN, JOE L.	2650	9281	1651	2518	449	96	268	1143	689	.427	1865	1015	.271
MORRIS, JOHN	39	100	8	24	0	1	1	14	6	.290	7	15	.240
MORYN, WALT	785	2506	324	667	116	16	101	354	7	.446	251	393	.266
MUMPHREY, JERRY	1404	4618	616	1330	196	53	57	522	173	.390	436	625	.288
MUSIAL, STAN	3026	10972	1949	3630	725	177	475	1951	78	.559	1599	696	.331
NARRON, SAM	24	28	0	8	0	0	0	1	0	.286	1	2	.286
NELSON, ROCKY	620	1394	186	347	61	14	31	173	7	.379	130	94	.249
NIEMAN, BOB	1113	3452	455	1018	180	32	125	544	10	.474	435	512	.295
NIETO, TOM	158	404	27	94	17	3	4	53	0	.319	37	76	.233
NOREN, IRV	1093	3119	443	857	157	35	65	453	34	.410	335	350	.275
NORTHEY, RON	1084	3172	385	874	172	28	108	513	7	.450	361	297	.276
NOSSEK, JOE	295	579	47	132	25	4	3	53	8	.301	19	72	.228
O'BRIEN, JOHNNY	339	815	90	204	35	5	4	59	2	.320	59	82	.250
OBERKFELL, KEN	1059	3423	408	970	169	36	20	303	54	.371	414	253	.283
OLIVARES, ED	24	35	2	5	0	0	0	1	1	.143	0	7	.143
OLIVER, GENE	786	2216	268	546	111	5	93	320	24	.427	215	420	.246
OQUENDO, JOSE	277	655	72	153	16	1	1	40	20	.266	49	106	.234
PAPI, STAN	225	523	49	114	26	6	7	51	2	.331	24	99	.278
PARIS, KELLY	68	149	14	33	6	0	0	8	8	.262	15	29	.221
PENA, GEORGE	No major league statistics												
PENDLETON, TERRY	375	1399	149	357	58	11	7	161	61	.327	87	166	.255
PHILLIPS, MIKE	712	1719	166	412	46	24	11	145	12	.314	133	242	.240
PINSON, VADA	2469	9645	1366	2757	485	127	256	1170	305	.442	574	1196	.286
PORTER, DARRELL	1697	5409	746	1338	234	48	181	805	39	.409	875	982	.247
PORTER, J.W.	229	544	58	124	22	1	8	62	4	.316	53	96	.228
QUIRK, JAMIE	534	1188	100	286	58	4	23	125	3	354	63	228	.241
RADER, DAVE	846	2405	254	619	107	12	30	235	8	.349	245	180	.257
RAJSICH, GARY	98	205	23	55	11	3	3	17	1	.395	22	42	.268
RAMIREZ, MILT	94	152	14	28	3	2	0	6	0	.230	13	18	.184
RAMSEY, MIKE	385	771	80	187	25	6	2	57	14	.298	46	107	.243
RAND, DICK	72	146	11	35	3	1	2	13	0	.315	14	31	.240
RAPP, VERN	No major league statistics												
RAYFORD, FLOYD	370	994	107	244	43	1	36	114	4	.399	53	216	.245
REESE, JIMMIE	232	742	123	206	39	4	8	70	7	.373	48	37	.278

PLAYER (continued)

PLAYER	G	AB	R	H	2B	3B	HR	RBI	SB	SLG	BB	SO	AVG
REITZ, KEN	1344	4777	366	1243	243	12	68	548	10	.359	184	518	.260
REPULSKI, RIP	928	3088	407	830	153	23	106	416	25	.436	207	433	.269
RICE, DEL	1309	3826	342	908	177	20	79	441	1	.356	382	522	.237
RICE, HAL	424	1183	129	307	52	12	19	162	2	.372	94	133	.260
RICHARD, LEE	239	492	71	103	12	6	2	29	12	.270	33	77	.209
RICKETTS, DAVE	130	213	15	53	9	0	1	20	0	.305	10	23	.249
ROJAS, COOKIE	1822	6309	714	1660	254	25	54	593	74	.337	396	489	.263
ROJEK, STAN	522	1764	225	470	67	13	4	122	32	.326	152	100	.266
ROMANO, JOHNNY	905	2767	355	706	112	10	129	417	7	.443	414	485	.255
ROOF, GENE	48	90	17	24	8	1	0	6	0	.356	14	23	.267
ROQUE, JORGE	65	139	14	19	4	1	2	12	4	.223	10	40	.137
RUDOLPH, KEN	328	743	55	158	23	2	6	64	2	.273	52	121	.213
SADOWSKI, BOB F.	184	329	38	73	9	3	7	46	3	.331	33	63	.222
SALAS, MARK	225	638	80	170	28	9	17	75	3	.418	36	72	.266
SANCHEZ, ORLANDO	74	110	11	24	3	2	0	12	1	.282	7	19	.218
SANTANA, RAFAEL	374	1089	94	267	41	3	3	71	1	.295	76	116	.245
SARNI, BILL	390	1182	107	311	50	11	22	151	6	.380	89	135	.263
SAUER, HANK	1399	4796	709	1278	200	19	288	876	11	.496	561	714	.266
SAVAGE, TED	642	1375	202	321	51	11	34	163	49	.361	200	272	.233
SAWATSKI, CARL	633	1449	133	351	46	5	58	213	2	.401	191	251	.242
SCHAFFER, JIMMIE	304	574	53	128	28	3	11	56	3	.340	49	127	.223
SCHEFFING, BOB	517	1357	105	357	53	9	20	187	6	.360	127	127	.263
SCHEINBLUM, RICHIE	462	1218	131	320	52	9	13	127	9	.352	149	135	.263
SCHOENDIENST, RED	2216	8479	1223	2449	427	78	84	773	89	.387	606	346	.289
SCHOFIELD, J. DICK	1321	3083	394	699	113	20	21	211	12	.297	390	526	.227
SCOTT, TONY	991	2803	331	699	111	28	17	253	125	.327	186	464	.249
SEXTON, JIMMY	236	372	53	81	9	3	5	24	36	.298	32	71	.218
SHANNON, MIKE	882	2780	313	710	116	23	68	367	19	.387	224	525	.255
SIMMONS, TED	2305	8396	1048	2402	469	47	242	1348	20	.440	819	662	.286
SIMPSON, DICK	288	518	94	107	19	2	15	56	10	.338	64	174	.207
SISLER, DICK	799	2606	302	720	118	28	55	360	6	.406	226	253	.276
SIZEMORE, TED	1411	5011	577	1311	188	21	23	430	59	.321	469	350	.262
SKINNER, BOB	1381	4318	642	1198	197	58	103	531	67	.421	485	646	.277
SLAUGHTER, ENOS	2380	7946	1247	2383	413	148	169	1304	71	.453	1019	538	.300
SMITH, BOBBY GENE	476	962	101	234	35	5	13	96	5	.331	55	154	.243
SMITH, CHARLIE	1324	3848	363	950	158	19	69	374	13	.367	201	535	.247
SMITH, HAL R.	570	1697	126	437	63	4	23	172	6	.345	102	128	.258
SMITH, KEITH	53	111	17	23	3	0	0	8	2	.306	6	10	.207
SMITH, LONNIE	909	3148	571	915	166	37	41	289	299	.406	326	458	.291
SMITH, OZZIE	1317	4739	583	1169	179	38	13	374	303	.309	528	305	.247
SMITH, REGGIE	1987	7033	1123	2020	363	57	314	1092	137	.489	890	1030	.287
SPEIER, CHRIS	2039	6631	698	1634	276	49	98	661	35	.347	777	889	.246
SPENCER, DARYL	1098	3689	457	901	145	20	105	428	13	.380	449	516	.244
SPIEZIO, ED	554	1544	126	367	56	4	39	174	16	.355	135	245	.238
STALLCUP, VIRGIL	587	2059	171	497	99	13	22	214	9	.334	51	181	.241
STANKY, EDDIE	1259	4301	811	1154	185	35	29	364	48	.348	996	374	.268
STEIN, BILL	959	2811	268	751	135	18	44	311	16	.370	186	413	.267
STINSON, BOB	652	1634	166	408	61	7	33	180	8	.356	201	254	.250
STOCK, MILT	1628	6249	839	1806	270	57	22	696	155	.361	455	321	.289
SUTHERLAND, GARY	1031	3104	308	754	109	10	24	239	11	.308	207	219	.243
SWISHER, STEVE	509	1414	108	305	49	7	20	124	4	.303	118	322	.216
TAMARGO, JOHN	135	244	19	59	12	1	4	33	1	.348	34	27	.242
TATE, LEE	51	85	9	14	3	1	1	5	0	.259	9	10	.165
TAUSSIG, DON	153	263	38	69	14	5	4	30	2	.399	21	53	.262
TAYLOR, CARL	411	846	113	225	31	6	10	115	12	.352	136	130	.266
TAYLOR, JOE	119	297	34	74	16	1	9	31	0	.401	28	61	.249
TEMPLETON, GARRY	1423	5562	703	1578	240	86	44	519	215	.382	256	773	.284
TENACE, GENE	1555	4390	653	1060	200	20	201	674	36	.429	984	998	.241
THACKER, MOE	158	260	20	46	7	0	2	20	1	.227	40	81	.177
TOLAN, BOB	1282	4238	572	1121	173	34	86	497	193	.382	258	587	.265

PLAYER	G	AB	R	H	2B	3B	HR	RBI	SB	SLG	BB	SO	AVG
TORRE, JOE	2209	7874	996	2342	344	59	252	1185	10	.452	779	1094	.297
TYSON, MIKE	1017	2959	281	714	118	28	27	269	23	.327	175	411	.241
UECKER, BOB	297	731	65	146	22	0	14	74	0	.287	96	167	.200
URIBE, JOSE	312	948	96	218	35	5	6	72	31	.296	91	135	.230
VAN SLYKE, ANDY	521	1512	205	392	79	22	41	204	104	.422	203	274	.259
VIRDON, BILL	1583	5980	735	1596	237	81	91	502	47	.379	442	647	.267
VOSS, BILL	475	1177	119	267	29	10	19	127	15	.317	117	167	.227
WAGNER, LEON	1352	4426	636	1202	150	32	211	669	32	.455	435	656	.272
WALKER, HARRY	807	2651	385	786	126	37	10	214	42	.383	245	175	.296
WALLER, TY	52	104	17	25	2	1	0	14	2	.385	7	28	.240
WARWICK, CARL	530	1462	168	363	51	10	40	149	13	.360	127	241	.248
WESTLAKE, WALLY	958	3117	474	848	107	33	127	539	19	.450	317	453	.272
WHISENANT, PETE	475	988	140	221	46	8	37	134	17	.399	86	196	.224
WHITE, BILL	1673	5972	843	1706	278	65	202	870	103	.455	596	927	.286
WHITE, JERRY	621	1170	154	300	50	9	20	106	57	.366	146	174	.256
WHITFIELD, FRED	817	2284	242	578	93	8	108	356	7	.443	139	371	.253
WICKER, FLOYD	81	113	10	18	1	0	1	6	0	.195	7	33	.159
WILBER, DEL	299	720	67	174	35	7	9	115	1	.389	44	96	.242
WILLIAMS, JIMY	14	13	1	3	0	0	0	1	0	.231	1	6	.231
YOUNG, BOBBY	687	2447	244	609	68	28	15	137	18	.318	208	212	.249
YOUNGBLOOD, JOEL	1180	3327	419	890	168	23	74	382	58	.399	304	538	.268
YVARS, SAL	210	418	41	102	12	0	10	42	1	.344	37	41	.244